101 Circus Games for Children

SmartFun Books from Hunter House

101

Circus Games for Children

Juggling — Clowning — Balancing Acts —
Acrobatics — Animal Numbers

Paul Rooyackers

Translated by Amina Marix Evans
Illustrated by Geert Snijders

A Hunter House SmartFun Book

Hunter House Inc., Publishers
PO Box 2914
Alameda CA 94501-0914

Library of Congress Cataloging-in-Publication Data

Rooyackers, Paul.
101 circus games for children : juggling—clowning—balancing acts—
acrobatics—animal numbers / Paul Rooyackers, translated by Amina Marix Evans,
illustrated by Geert Snijders.
p.   cm.
ISBN 978-0-89793-516-6 (pbk.) — ISBN 978-0-89793-517-3 (spiral)
1. Games.   2. Circus.   3. Group games.   4. Amusements.
I. Marix Evans, Amina.   II. Title.
GV1199.R66 2009
791.3—dc22   2009024382

Project Credits

Cover Design Jil Weil and Stefanie Gold
Illustrations Geert Snijders
Translator Amina Marix Evans
Book Production John McKercher
Developmental and Copy Editor Amy Bauman
Proofreader Herman Leung
Editor Alexandra Mummery
Senior Marketing Associate Reina Santana
Publicity Associate Sean Harvey
Rights Coordinator Candace Groskreutz
Customer Service Manager Christina Sverdrup
Order Fulfillment Washul Lakdhon
Administrator Theresa Nelson
Computer Support Peter Eichelberger
Publisher Kiran S. Rana

Printed and bound by Bang Printing, Brainerd, Minnesota

Manufactured in the United States of America

9 8 7 6 5 4 3 2 1   First Edition   10 11 12 13 14

Contents

A list of the games, divided by age groups, begins on the next page.

*Please note that the illustrations in this book are all outline drawings.
The fact that the pages are white does not imply that the people all have
white skin. This book is for people of all races and ethnic identities.*

List of Games

Games for 4–7-Year-Olds

Games for 7–9-Year-Olds

Games for 9–10-Year-Olds

Important Note

The material in this book is intended to provide information about a safe, enjoyable program of physical games for children to play. Every effort has been made to provide accurate and dependable information. The contents of this book have been compiled through professional research and in consultation with professionals. However, professionals have differing opinions, and some of the information may become outdated; therefore, the publisher, authors, and editors, as well as the professionals quoted in the book, cannot be held responsible for any error, omission, or dated material. The authors and publisher assume no responsibility for any outcome of applying the information in this book. Follow the instructions closely. Note, too, that children's bodies differ, and no one should assume or be forced to assume any physical positions that cause pain or discomfort. If you have questions concerning an exercise or the application of the information described in this book, please consult a qualified medical professional.

Introduction

This book contains 101 circus games for children 4 years of age and up. There are several introductory exercises especially for the youngest members of the group. With these games, you can put together a complete circus show and make a presentation.

101 Circus Games for Children is intended for use with anyone wanting to learn to play, act, or present; those who are enthralled by the circus; and those working with children 4 to 12 years old. The book was also created with the idea of encouraging teachers and group leaders to use games in the context of a circus performance. These games have not been published elsewhere.

The games vary in form and content and increase in difficulty in accordance with the age groups indicated.

Target Group

101 Circus Games for Children includes many types of games that can be used by teachers in the creative arts, activity leaders, producers of children's theater, and those in charge of open days.

Many of the games can be adapted as independent presentations. Or several of them from different parts of the book can be combined to create a complete circus performance. The games have proven suitable for parents' evenings, school evenings, and workweeks. They can also be used to develop children's enjoyment of games as well as their understanding of teamwork.

This book is one of a series of educational games books published by Hunter House. In common with other books in the series, this book also consists of two parts. In the first part, we concentrate on the aims of games, the components of a circus, and on the didactic qualities that can be important for a group leader in transforming games and ideas into a circus presentation. Part two consists of the descriptions of the games, divided into the following age groups: 4–7 years, 7–9 years, 9–10 years, and 10–12 years.

For reasons of readability, the book is written varying the pronouns, sometimes using "he" and other times using "she" or "they." Of course, every "he" implies a "she," and vice versa.

The Circus—The First Impression

The circus is in town! A man on an elephant leads a street parade while some clowns pass out flyers. A truck blares out circus music, and in the distance you can see the colors of the Big Top tent and the animal trailers parked around it.

Nearing the circus grounds, you can see the animals pacing nervously in their cages. Clowns run back and forth, collecting a few last things from the caravans and carrying them back to the Big Top. At the entrance, you can see people who you later recognize in the ring. You stand in line for the tickets outside, maybe in the rain. And maybe also by the orchestra playing as the audience files into the huge tent.

A child going to the circus for the first time may be overwhelmed by the atmosphere: the lights, the sound of a trumpet, the festive atmosphere, the smell of the animals, the sight of the first clown, the smell of the wooden seats, the sawdust, the smell of popcorn and other food.

Where Does the Word Circus Come From?

The circus got its name centuries ago from the *Circus Maximus* of the Roman Empire. *Circus* means "a circle or a ring" and *maximus* means "the greatest."

A traveling circus is often smaller than a circus that does not travel, unless it is going to a big city. Circuses that go to small towns and villages have to adapt to the size of the ground available to them to pitch the big tent. In ancient Roman times, the circus was more about chariot racing held in front of huge crowds. The 1959 film *Ben Hur* features a reconstruction of a circus of this kind and in the same arena where the gladiators would fight for their lives.

The circus as we know it today is of another kind that has existed for just a couple of hundred years. This type of circus is generally made up of families who travel around, complete with tent, animals, trapeze artists, trucks, and caravans. In this sort of circus, you will find that animals are making way for other kinds of entertainment. Look at the Cirque du Soleil, for instance. It has no animals, but it does have plenty of clowns, jugglers, acrobats, and virtuosos of all kinds.

Since the advent of circus schools in the 1980s, the circus has changed considerably. The *nouveau cirque* came into being in Canada. It was a school where young artistes could work on their acts. This resulted in the formation of the Cirque du Soleil, which has since grown into a billion-dollar business. This kind of circus stands in stark contrast to the small family circuses where everyone has to pitch in just for the business to survive.

The New Circus

The old-fashioned circus with animals, clowns, trapeze artists, an orchestra, and all that old-world glory is almost a thing of the past. These days everything has to glisten and shine. Modern flyers are full of exaggerated claims, such as "the world's best slack-rope dancer," "the most romantic air ballet," "the best Australian boomerang throwers," "the most supple ballet dancers," and "3,000-year-old Greek acrobatics"—next to the obligatory "fiercest lion in the world." The circus evolves with time, and, in order for it to survive, people need to come up with new ideas all the time.

The new circus no longer needs a tent for the performers. It can take place in the street as street theater. These developments have led to the introduction of many street festivals.

The Aim of Circus Games

This book features a number of games in which drama is the most important element.

These games are designed to

- be relaxing
- encourage creativity
- help develop each child's personality
- encourage children's social and emotional development
- invite children to give a physical shape to words
- help children build confidence in their use of language and their bodies

For a further development of these aims, I suggest you look at *101 Drama Games for Children,* which is an earlier book in this series.

As you experiment with the games, still more goals will become apparent. As a group leader working with young participants, you need to be conscious of the aims above and be aware of which goal you are working on in each situation. Make sure to identify the goal for yourself with each new exercise you introduce. Ask yourself: Does this game suit the group? Can the children do it successfully? Always ask first, "What am I trying to achieve?"

Supervising the Games

Supervising a game when you are working with children means that you have to keep your ears and eyes open all the time. For this reason, it is a good idea to structure the session. This can also ensure that you don't get unpleasant surprises.

With all the games in this book, as noted below, the absolute priority has to be the safety of the participants and the audience. There should not be a single moment where anyone is in danger. And for all the games the first rule is: Test it yourself first to be sure that it works.

What Is Important?

1. Ensure the safety of the participants and the audience.
2. Make sure the space in which you are working is quiet.
3. Make an agreement with the group about when group members can speak and when they need to keep quiet.
4. Make rules about criticizing each other (see "Rules of the Game" on page 5).
5. Make sure that both the players and the audience are concentrating.
6. Tell the players on what they should focus.

Practical Tips

Some groups can sort themselves out. Some participants can easily adapt to a new group or a new pairing depending on who is present. But this is not true across the board.

Putting Together Pairs or Groups

Often children in younger age groups, in order to feel secure, prefer to stick with their friends. And "best friends" are an important concept at this age. But to keep the children from forming cliques and exclusive friendships, it is a good idea to keep finding new ways of dividing the class into groups or pairs.

If the leader is always finding different ways of dividing the group, the children will happily go along with it. Here are a few suggestions:

- Ask what everyone has in their backpacks or desks and divide the group accordingly. You can also divide them by the color of their shoelaces or their type of shoes.
- Divide the group by the colors of the clothes people are wearing.
- Divide the group on the basis of hair length and hair color.
- Divide the group on the basis of a good mix of girls and boys.
- Divide the group on the basis of height.
- Divide the group on the basis of names that start with the same letter.
- With enough different ways to split the group, you can make endless combinations.

The Group Leader's Signal

In the course of a game, it is important that the leader establishes clear signals to start the game or to interrupt it if things are not going well. The leader needs to devise signals for each phase of the game so that the group can react immediately. It is a good idea to make specific signals to start and stop the games simply as part of the leader's daily ritual. A whistle or a snap of the fingers works if the group is accustomed to it. Dropping your voice to a whisper works, too, but, again, only if the group is used to it. You might also want to make safety signals, and signals to speed up one act or announce the next might also be useful.

A leader who does not yet know the group he is working with is advised to introduce the signals and rules during the very first class. The participants need to have a clear signal for when the leader wants their attention and on which to begin the game. One possible series of signals could be:

- Give the "Is the public ready?" sign, followed by a verbal: "Audience ready?"
- Give the "Are the players ready?" sign, followed by a verbal: "Players ready?"
- The leader gives no sign but says, "Play!"

If the leader always sticks to the same method of starting, the group will pick up on the process quickly and follow along more accurately.

Rules of the Game

As group leader, you will want to take note of the following guidelines:

- Never begin a game until it is quiet. That way, everyone can concentrate on understanding the aim of the game and how it is done.
- Make clear when the participants should work on their own and when they need guidance.
- Teach the participants to listen to the leader and to each other. Listening and allowing people to express themselves increases the pace and the enjoyment of the game.
- If someone is performing, no one should make comments, walk away, or otherwise disturb the action. A group leader will want to strictly enforce this rule as concentration is very important to helping the players remain in their roles.
- Criticism is permissible as long as it is creative and constructive. Teach the participants to ask questions about the presentations. Asking questions always works positively, which will help the group avoid negative

comments. The leader should intervene immediately if she sees that someone is taking a negative approach.

- Participants generally have good insight into what they themselves experience as negative. The same goes for the way they experience the presentation. The leader should ask about their experiences and decide whether a rule or the form of a game needs to be adapted.

- Close a presentation with silence or some other clear rounding-off that everyone will recognize. This could be a final few words, a signal, a thought about the dialogue or the way it was played (by different participants in turn), an evaluation, or a debriefing.

Key to the Icons Used in the Exercises

To help you find exercises suitable for a particular situation, the games are divided into categories for four age groups. Each game also is coded with symbols, or icons, that tell you the following things about the activity at a glance:

- the recommended age of the participants
- the time necessary for the game
- the size of the group needed
- if an assistant is required
- if a large space is required
- if physical contact is or might be involved
- if a game is potentially dangerous
- if props are required
- if a musical accompaniment is suggested

These icons are explained in more detail below.

The recommended age of the participants. Each game belongs in a different age-group category, but in practice many of the games for younger players are also suitable for older children. Many of the games also are adaptable and can be made to suit a different age group. A minimum age recommendation is given for each game, using this icon:

 = Recommended minimum age of participants

The time necessary for the game. It takes a little while to learn and practice an act. If all the participants study the same act and the group leader knows how long the act should take, then it is easy to estimate how long the rehearsals will take.

If the leader knows the group well, she also can see if the same act or game can be repeated for another presentation or if the circus game can be built on or switched out for another kind of game.

Note that when the time necessary spans a range of time, the lower limit will be indicated in the icon and a plus sign will appear in the middle of the clockface.

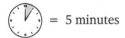 = 5 minutes

= 15 minutes

= 120 minutes

= one hour or more

= 45-minute activity that can be repeated in multiple meetings of a group/class

The size of the group needed. You can play most of the games in this book with a group of any size. Those exercises that require pairs or a specific number of participants will be marked with one of the following icons:

 = Participants play in groups of [xx]

 = Participants play in pairs

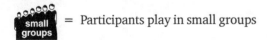 = Participants play in small groups

If an assistant is required. When performing some circus games with young children, you may need to use extra assistants. Acrobatics in particular require additional helpers as young children are very enthusiastic and may do tricks they are not yet trained to do. When you explain a more difficult game, make sure the children do not try it by themselves if the instructions suggest they need someone to help them.

 = Assistant required

If a large space is required. Almost all of the exercises in this book may be practiced in a relatively small space. However, a large space is ideal for some of the exercises, especially if you have a group of three or more people. The activities that require a larger space when a group is involved are marked with this icon:

 = Large space required

For more about space considerations see the "Workspace Needed" section on page 15.

If physical contact is or might be involved. Although a certain amount of body contact might be acceptable in certain environments, the following icon has been inserted at the top of any exercise that might involve anything from a small amount of contact to minor collisions. You can figure out in advance if the activity is suitable for your participants and/or environment.

 = Physical contact

If a game is potentially dangerous. Safety is of the utmost importance, and the leader should be very careful when gauging which games in the book will be appropriate for their particular situation, as organizations have different rules about what types of activities are acceptable and the maturity levels of children vary widely. If there is a potential that a particular game could be dangerous if not performed carefully and with supervision, the following icon will be listed at the top of the game:

 = Game is potentially dangerous

If props are required. Many of the games need no special props. Where you need to use balls, ropes, cords, or scenery (such as chairs or a chest with props), this is indicated.

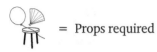 = Props required

If a musical accompaniment is suggested. Many exercises in this book would be enhanced significantly by music. The games for which music is strongly suggested are marked with the following icon. If a specific type of music is recommended, the game will say so.

 = Music suggested

Performance/Presentation

Once a circus group has rehearsed a number of acts, you can prepare the participants for a presentation. As you craft the presentation, make sure there is plenty
of variety in the program—acrobatics, clowning, juggling, an orchestra, a presenter, and maybe even an act involving a pet. Work on diversity from the start;
it makes the show!

Think about how long the first show should be. Work with the participants
and decide which acts they are confident enough to perform in public. It is no fun
to perform an act that does not work well. This is particularly true of circus acts,
where the audience expects things to go like clockwork.

A key role to any program is the ringmaster. He or she carries the show, and
a really good ringmaster can even rescue an act that completely messes up. But
whether or not the ringmaster is called upon to save the show, his performance
needs to propel the show along. With young participants, the presenter is the
person who can put right anything that goes wrong and give the whole program
a positive direction.

Much of what is said about the importance of the ringmaster also can be said
of the orchestra or the recorded music chosen. Upbeat music propels the performance and gives it tempo.

Another important consideration is the running order of the presentation.
For example, leaders will want to stagger the entr'actes, sometimes also known
as interludes, which are those performances, such as the clowns, that fill in the
spaces between acts and ensure that other performers have time to change costumes. In addition, you will want to interweave fast numbers and slow ones, alternate acrobatics with poetry, contrast the verbosity of a clown with the silence
of the juggler. Circus is also a mix of the traditional and exotic; there are certain
acts that will always be a part of the circus—like the sad clown—but also acts
like the "painted canary that can do ventriloquism" from Afghanistan. Keeping
track of the order will allow the audience to hold their breath in one act and find
relaxation in a slow number. To give the audience a moment to switch gears,
you could even have someone offering snacks if you want.

Organizing a Circus Project

Putting a circus program together might sound simple, but there are a lot of details that need arranging. If you are presenting your program at school, you will need the gym or auditorium available for several days for rehearsals and decoration.

If you are working outside in a tent, you first need to decide how big the tent needs to be: there must be plenty of space for the audience so they can see; the artistes have to enter from one side and be able to leave from the other side. All the artistes need to be able to wait behind the tent until it is time for their act.

This means that you need a stage manager whose job it is to make sure that the acts are ready and go on at the right moment. You need a manager for the stage or arena, but you might also need one behind the scenes. Who gives out the props and who brings back props from the arena so that the program maintains its tempo? The fact that so many extra people are needed when working with children is a good thing because there are always kids who don't want to perform in public but who are very good at doing hair, makeup, cleaning up, etc.

One more necessary thought: Make sure you have a first-aid kit, and someone who knows a little about using first aid. (You never know.)

Logistics Training

Give the sign for the show to begin when you are certain that everything is ready. This is another thing you train the participants for in the last few rehearsals. This logistics training is something you can do several times with the production crew.

This can also be done without the performers present or simply without people in costume. That is called a "dry run," and during a dry run you simply rehearse the cues linking one act to the next. For example, what are the last words the clown says or what is the last trick the juggler does before they change over? Make a list of the cues so you know when the acts are approaching the end and it is time for the next act to get ready to come on.

When everything is going well with the production crew, do a run through with the cast. Try it the first time with the performers wearing their regular clothes; simply practice the entrances and exits and the order in which they come. Undoubtedly you will find that one act will need much more preparation than another and that you will be able to rehearse the whole show several times if you don't have to deal with all the costumes and props. Regardless of that, however, doing a run-through of the program will give you insight into what you need and when.

The Props List

With a few children and some adults, make lists of all the things you are going to need. The list should include things to buy, things to make, and items that need to be moved.

Then comes the moment when you must decide the precise order of the show. Once that is set, you can create a list of all the props that are needed for each act and the order in which they need to be taken on and off the stage.

Who does what in each act? That's another crucial question. Make notes for each act and add in the cues (at what moment the final sentence is spoken or the final action is done) for transition into the next act.

The Dress Rehearsal

The dress rehearsal is an opportunity to sort out a number of matters. Included among these are:

- the tent or decorated room
- the lighting, preferably with many possibilities from colored footlights to hanging spots
- the sound system
- the cue list
- the costume list
- the props list
- the orchestra and orchestra space
- sheet music, if needed, and a list of the pieces to be performed
- the ring
- sheets to hang around the ring
- the ringmaster
- the cashier
- the snack seller
- artistes
- dressing rooms
- cages for small animals, if required
- extra helpers for preparing acts backstage
- technicians for sound and lighting

- the stage manager (who coordinates and organizes everything back-stage and onstage)

Finales

There are certain numbers that, as you rehearse them, you will find will be best saved as finales. This could be because of the need to move a lot of props or because of the nature of the act itself. A few thoughts on that:

- Some acts are best suited for opening a program; others serve better for closing it.
- Never finish with a sad number or act; always close with an upbeat note. That's the circus!
- The most spectacular number should come right at the end.

The final performance is when all the artistes come back on stage one more time. Preferably this is in conjunction with an act in which all of the performers can take part.

Who Organizes What?

We have already mentioned the stage manager as the person who organizes everything. You will also need a producer to coordinate the entire performance. This person organizes all the arrangements and makes sure they are adhered to.

There is a preparation period before each individual performance. That means that there needs to be a written timetable in which each performance is listed along with its run time. Start with the following tasks and considerations to create this timetable:

1. Write down all the acts.
2. Make a program.
3. How long is each act?
4. How long are the changes between the acts?
5. Is the program in balance?
6. Which entr'actes are available to fill in the spaces?
7. Have the presentation's financial matters—as well as the program it-self—been sorted out?
8. Is there a list of all the tasks?
9. Make a list of addresses, phone numbers, and e-mail addresses for everyone involved.

10. Make a scenario and divide it into sections with a block for each act. The types of information gathered here should include:

- Who is in it?
- Which props are needed?
- Who will put them in position?
- Which music goes with each act?
- What kind of lighting is needed?
- Which microphones need to be open?

The Circus Games

A Description of the Circus Games

As mentioned earlier, the games are divided into categories for four age groups. Several games from these categories can be combined to create a performance piece. That is just one option and is not essential, of course, because each game can be practiced and performed independently of the others. Each game also has its own lesson to teach and trains the players in how to interpret circus acts.

Start with short simple games from the series for the youngest players in order to allow the participants to get used to practicing and performing the various acts. Very often, after doing a simple act, participants will want to move on to a more complicated version.

Sometimes the games themselves include variations in the way each can be interpreted or performed. This frequently involves taking things to another level.

Workspace Needed

A gym or game room is suitable for most of the games, but in some cases a game works better in a dedicated space—on the stage, for instance. It is helpful if the work space has as few distracting decorations as possible. An empty space is ideal for all games—especially from a safety point of view. Many players find an atmospheric space pleasant (dark curtains hung around the room with a circus ring around the outside). An act can also be performed at a different location. An act can take on a completely different character when performed in the open air.

Clothing and Equipment Needed

For circus games, and in particular with acrobatics, it is good if you have some gym equipment such as mats, proper clothing, and other things. All children— even the youngest ones—should have special clothing set aside for doing acrobatics or outdoor exercises. Make sure that they have advance permission to get these clothes dirty! Also, if they do not work barefoot, they may need gym shoes or ballet shoes.

Circus Games for 4–7-Year-Olds

Children begin school at the age of 4. Until this point, many things were determined by their lives at home.

A child may go to the circus or to the zoo with his parents; she may play with her friends. With the family, children can discover family life, go on vacation, learn new things in their own way, all at a gentle pace and as part of your home life. Some will have learned to ride a bike—with or without training wheels—and to jump from the sofa or the stairs, again supported by their home situation.

At this age, children consider everything an experience; they love it or they are completely disinterested. It is either this child's "thing," or it isn't. A first visit to the circus may mean that the child becomes completely enchanted by the experience and immediately sees himself as a clown, an acrobat, or an animal trainer. It is a time of toys, where the child is driven by whatever she is given. Most children love stories, whether the stories are scary or have happy endings.

But as the child enters school, many things that were previously determined by their lives at home will change. They will begin to assert themselves and strive for independence. In regard to what you are trying to teach them, children will try to copy the exercises, not realizing how difficult they may be. At this age, they move consciously and unconsciously. But performing tricks is something that needs to be done very consciously and under the guidance of an adult who is able to foresee the dangers.

Also at this age, circus games are just that—games. The game is presented as part of a story, and that way it is more attractive to the children.

Circus Program for 4–7-Year-Olds

For 4–7-year-olds, you will automatically create a different performance from the one you would design for older children. For this age group, everything is practice, and you can avoid making the children nervous by talking about a serious performance. They just do it, and at the same time—while they are practicing—you can strive to increase their capacity for concentration. You do that in a number of ways including through the use of your voice, the addition of music, or with the help of assistants who can help if the participants' attention wanders. For the youngest children, a performance should not last more than half an hour, as they will not be able to concentrate for longer.

To keep the younger children's attention, you can break up the performances by including an entr'acte. As noted earlier, this is a short piece designed to switch the attention from a previous number; it is usually lighthearted in tone. During this interlude, the next number can be prepared.

What kind of performance can you create using the games described for this age group? First read the games through, try them out, and see if you can make something of the sequence described below.

The ringmaster comes in, thanks the audience for coming to this unique show, and introduces the first artistes:

1. Game #5: Look! No Hands!

2. Game #7: I Can Fly

3. Game #24: The Oversized Coat or Sweater (entr'acte #1)

4. Game #8: I Know a Trick

5. Game #9: Conveyor Belt

6. Game #16: Two Clowns (entr'acte #2)

7. Game #10: The Worm

8. Game #20: The Best Box-Stacking Clown (entr'acte #3)

9. Game #22: Falling with Boxes (entr'acte #4)

10. Game #13: Rolling

11. Game #14: Tricks with the Balance Beam

12. Game #15: Out of Balance

13. Game #23: Falling into the Box (entr'acte #5)

14. Game #18: On Top of Each Other

15. Game #12: Elastic Jersey Dancers

16. Game #25: A Bucket of Water (finale)

Then the curtain call: Everyone comes back in, bows to the audience, and receives applause.

Warming Up

The first game is about warming up, which is an essential part of circus games!

Instructions: The leader does a quick warm-up with the children that stretches and flexes a number of muscle groups. Say:

- *Rub your hands together, both the palms and the backs of your hands.*
- *With one fist, gently pound up and down the opposite arm. Switch to the other arm.*
- *Pound your legs gently with both fists, keeping your fists soft and loose. Then do the same with your tummy, chest, and back (as much as you can reach).*
- *Run in place to loosen up your feet.*
- *Jump gently—small jumps—sort of throwing yourself upward and letting yourself come back down.*
- *Walk around the room, allowing your arms to swing, completely relaxed. Gradually increase the speed until you are walking fast and really moving your arms.*
- *Coming to a stop, stand in place and jump up and down again. Slowly come to a complete stop.*

What's the Idea?

Instructions: The participants stand in a circle. The leader makes some movements (e.g., skating), and the class copies him. The movements begin normally but become gradually more and more exaggerated, and more and more clownish. Once participants realize all of the movements they can make, the leader picks different children and asks them to come up with a movement for the rest of the class to follow. Everyone copies the child, all moving together.

After a few times, the leader chooses another child to stand in the center of the circle and create another movement for the class to follow. With younger children, the leader may have to help them come up with different movements at first. After a while, though, it will be easier for the children to think of the movements themselves.

Variations:

- Ask the children to come up with movements that come from Warming Up (Game #1). They should involve stretching and flexing.

- A stretch-flex routine that the children have thought of themselves is even better.

Antonio Macaroni's Circus Family

Props: Chairs; caps and scarves; "circus" clothes; a camera (optional)

What does the Macaroni family look like? This Italian family of circus performers always wants to be first to sit on the chair when photos are being taken of the circus troupe.

Instructions: The "Macaroni family" consists of a father, a mother, and two children. The four of them will not fit on one chair together, but they still try....

Divide the class into groups of four, with each person taking on the role of one of the family members. Together, the children try to figure out how all four of them can get on one chair—sitting, lying, or…?

Note: You will want to watch that the children don't injure themselves as they try out various seating strategies. Safety is of the utmost importance, and you should be careful when gauging if this game is suitable for your particular situation.

4

The Chair Act from Napoli

Props: Strong chairs on which more than one person can stand

In the circus, you often see performers making pyramids or holding onto each other while one of them climbs on an object.

Instructions: Have the children each choose a partner. You should also choose a partner so you can model the game. Following your lead, children, in pairs, will climb a chair to make a "statue"—as if they are posing for a poster for the "Chair Act from Napoli." (Tell the children that the statue is to be an advertisement for the circus that is coming to town.) For moves that have participants leaning away from each other and the chair, show the children how to take hold of each other at the wrists (see the illustration below). This is a strong grip, so partners won't lose hold of each other.

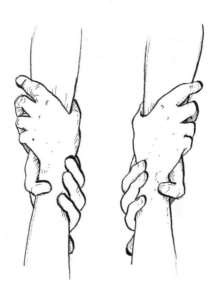

After the pairs have had time to work, invite several different pairs of children to present their statue to the group.

Tip: Do not expect young children to be able to work independently.

Note: Safety is of the utmost importance, and you should be careful when gauging if this game is suitable for your particular situation.

Look! No Hands!

Instructions: Have pairs of children sit on the ground back to back. Tell the children to pretend that they are glued together—without holding onto each other—no hands. They then try to rise from sitting to standing. Not everyone will be able to do this; partners will have to work together very closely. It usually works best if the partners breathe out as they push upward, making a sound as they do. Ask the participants: *Can you find different ways of getting to a standing position? Clowns come up with new ideas every day, so you can too!*

Remind the class to keep their arms hanging loosely by their sides.

Balance

Keeping balance is very important for a circus performer. Tell the children that balance is something they need to practice.

Instructions: Divide the class into pairs. With small children, it is good to work with assistants because balance needs to be explained demonstrating on a child in position.

Partners stand face to face, holding each other by the wrists.

Tell them to place their feet so they are touching their partner's feet. They have to hang on to each other to make that possible. If they can't do that, then let player Number 1 be the pillar, and player Number 2 can hang. Number 1 braces himself, standing with knees bent and legs slightly apart. Then Number 2 hangs, gently, until he can't go any further. Number 2 then comes back to the original position, and the players switch roles.

Variation: Player Number 2 puts his feet between those of Number 1.

I Can Fly

Prop: Rope

The circus often includes trapeze artists who fly through the air. This is also known as aerial acrobatics.

Instructions: In the gym, build a course that allows someone to fly through the air with the help of ropes. A line of mats under the ropes will ensure soft landings.

Ropes should be fixed so that, at their lowest point, the children "fly" just above the ground. If there are no ropes, skipping ropes can be used to make a rigging that the children can swing on to get the feeling of flying. Swinging on a low-slung rope a distance of a few feet and then jumping onto a soft surface can also feel like a circus act for a small child. You and your assistants can also hold children as they "fly" on the rope. Be sure to help with the landing, too.

I Know a Trick

Each child can think up a trick to do in front of the class. It could be a roll, a special jump, a backward summersault, putting a foot next to her ear, standing on one leg and blowing her nose. Ask a different child to come up with a new trick each class, and you will see more and more creativity developing. As the leader, do a trick of your own first.

Conveyor Belt

Imagine six or so participants lying close together on the ground on their stomachs, arms and legs stretched out, heads down. One child lies on top of the others, lengthwise, and moves and rolls as the row begins to move and roll in the same direction. As the group moves around the room in one direction, that participant on top will also roll along. Children love doing this "conveyor-belt" trick.

Instructions: Have the children practice rolling together in the same direction as if they are all stuck together. Once they have that down, have them try the movement again with someone lying on top, rolling along.

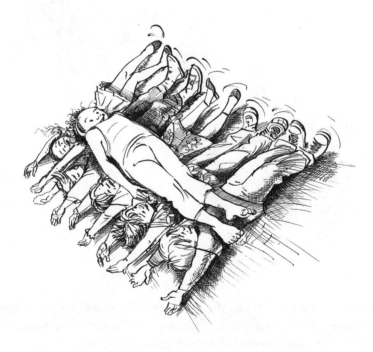

Tip: The child on top should, of course, remove her shoes and any other clothing or jewelry that could hurt the others.

The Worm

Instructions: To make a worm, you need four to five participants joined together. This can be achieved by having the children line up one behind the other on hands and knees. Have the children bend arms out at the elbow, stretch their legs back, and then clamp their knees around the person behind them so that only their hands are touching the ground. The worm can move if everyone walks on their hands—in the same tempo!

Variation: This exercise can also be turned into a game. Ask the children: *In how many different ways can you make a worm like this?* Then it can also become a clowning act, especially if it goes wrong a few times.

What Animal Is This?

Props: Large sheets of cloth

Working together with several participants, you can use your bodies to create an animal. Everyone knows the stereotypical depiction of an elephant: You put one hand around the other arm and then on your nose, and the other arm that dangles is the trunk. You can't really put any acrobatics with that, but if you have a big sheet, you can make the animal appear much larger. If you have stilts, you could even make a giraffe.

Instructions: Have the participants try making an animal with three people—a lion, for instance. Two people line up next to each other on hands and knees, forming a table, and the third person sits on their backs on hands and knees, distributing his weight evenly between the two "supporters." Ask the participants first to think of what animal they want to make and then to try drawing it. Once they have done that, they can try it out with the group.

Elastic
Jersey Dancers

Props: Double-stretch jersey tubes 5 feet long and wide enough to fit a person, preferably in dark colors

Music: Anything from Cirque du Soleil

Instructions: You can buy stretch jersey fabric at large home décor or crafts stores. Cut lengths of 5 feet, sew together the two longer ends, and leave the top and bottom ends open to create a cylinder. When you step inside the tube, you make a shape so that you look like some strange creature—especially if you can't see a head, arms, or legs anymore. If you want to, you could close the top with Velcro. You can act out the arrival of alien beings to the music; the Cirque du Soleil did this act in one of their shows, and the audience was amazed.

Rolling

Props: Gym mats

Children learn about rolling in their gym lessons. There they do somersaults, rolling forward over their heads, tucking them in well. Show the children that it is better to roll over a shoulder.

Instructions: To teach children how to do a roll, have them tuck in their shoulder, put an ear to the ground as if listening, then roll over their shoulder and onto their backs. This can be made part of a circus act by adding other "rolling" elements. For instance, one person (Number 2) lies on the ground and another performer (Number 1) does a roll over her. In the next step, Number 2 rolls on the ground toward Number 1, who does a shoulder roll over her. Now do the act with at least three people: Number 2 and Number 3 roll along the floor toward Number 1 (with some space between them). Number 1 rolls over Number 2, gets up and then rolls over Number 3, then stays on the ground and rolls in the same direction as Number 3. Meanwhile, Number 2 gets up and does a shoulder roll over Number 3 and then Number 1, and the game goes on. Number 3 then rolls over Number 1 and Number 2, etc.

Tricks with
the Balance Beam

Prop: A balance beam

Instructions: Schools and community centers often have benches. The underside may have a narrower beam. Turn the benches over to make a good balance beam for small children and some fun activities. The participants become tightrope walkers. This may quickly become boring for the 6–7-year-olds, so if you are working with this group, ask them to create tricks for two people on the bar.

Example: Two players approach each other from opposite ends. When they see that they can't pass each other, they go backward to their starting places.

Note: Safety is of the utmost importance, and you should be careful when gauging if this game is suitable for your particular situation.

Out of Balance

Props: A balance beam; objects for the player to carry, such as a balancing stick, one or more balls, cushions (*How many can you carry?*), one or more sandbags or beanbags, balloons, a tray of cups (plastic!), etc.

Instructions: To make balancing on the bar (from Game #14) more challenging, have the participants carry something with them. Clowns always find a way to make a zany act of something simple like this. Older participants will enjoy working on this aspect of the game.

Variation: Use a rope on the ground instead of a balance beam.

For beginners, balancing on even a slack rope on the ground is something of a handicap if they are also trying to carry things in their hands or arms.

Tip: Remind participants to place their feet sideways, especially on the rope. That way, they fall less easily.

Two Clowns

Props: Ropes (or a balance beam for older children); objects to carry (bags of groceries, boxes, balls, a potted plant—the sillier the better)

Instructions: Have pairs of children pretend to be two clowns—a clever one and a silly one who seems not so clever. The clever clown encourages the other to walk the rope carrying some extra things. Then the clever one will try to knock his friend off balance by startling her. But which clown is really the clever one?

Balance here is just a motive for the act. Is the rope broken perhaps? Does an alarm clock go off and scare whoever is on the rope? Does the phone ring for the person on the rope? The children can think up all kinds of reasons why the clown never manages to get to the other end of the rope with whatever he's carrying. Here, too, the children will enjoy creating an act with a story behind it.

The **Big Bench**

Props: Knee pads (optional)

Instructions: This game is designed for one adult and a child. The adult goes down on his hands and knees and forms a bench. The child can sit on the bench and get carried to the next spot. Instead of an adult you could use an older child—as long as one is strong enough to carry the other.

On Top of Each Other

Music (optional): Circus music or a drumroll, if possible

This is an exercise made for pairs of children. Have Number 1 get down on his hands and knees, and have Number 2 stand on the hips of Number 1. To do this, Number 2 supports herself with her hands on Number 1's shoulders and puts her feet one at a time on Number 1's back. Then she slowly lets go with her hands and stands up—supported by an assistant, if necessary. If Number 1 is up to it, the pair can then move along in this position for a few feet.

After a short display of balancing, the next pair takes the floor.

Tips:

- Partners should stand only on each other's pelvis. Make sure no one stands on the spine of the other!

- With small children, make sure there is always an assistant to help.

Note: Safety is of the utmost importance, and you should be careful when gauging if this game is suitable for your particular situation.

Boxes

Props: Boxes

Music (optional): Fast music

Instructions: Collect as many boxes as you can of all different sizes. Draw a chalk line on the floor to create a kind of course for participants to walk. Have each participant take a turn moving boxes. Who can move the most boxes along the course in the shortest time? Who can carry the most boxes without dropping them?

Tip: If this game will be used as part of an act, paint the boxes. For extra fun, paint yellow stars on a dark background or wrap the boxes in dark paper and apply the stars.

The Best
Box-Stacking Clown

Props: Clown noses (homemade) or face paint; lots of boxes; an award for the best box-stacking clown

Music (optional): Humorous circus music

Instructions: The purpose of this game is for a clown to pile up boxes in a different way from anyone else.

First have everyone make a clown nose or paint noses on their faces for them. To make clown noses, cut up an egg carton (or cartons). Paint each individual egg holder red and add a piece of elastic to go around the back of the clown's head.

The addition of noses will have an immediate effect on the atmosphere in the classroom. The youngest children will be especially excited about changing into the clown role once each of them has their own nose. And even the older children will be influenced by the addition of the noses, finding it easier to get into the part. Invite the younger children (or all of the children) to come to class dressed in clown's costumes.

To play the game, the leader will have to help the youngest clowns stack boxes. Have one clown try stacking a series of boxes. What story can the class invent so that the clown's stack of boxes ends up in one huge landslide?

Who can think of the most variations? This participant will receive the award for the best box-stacking clown. With the youngest group, you'll want everyone to get an award. For the older groups, try forming a panel of judges and have them choose the award winner. After 10 to 15 minutes, hold the award ceremony.

A Course in Falling

Props: Boxes; a drum and drumstick; cymbals; gym mats

Music: Drumrolls, cymbal clashes

A clown who is about to fall over delays it as long as he can. It looks as if he is about to fall from the start, but then, at the last moment, he doesn't.

Instructions: The leader starts by giving a "course in falling." Use the gym mats for this part of the exercise so that no one gets hurt.

    Before teaching this stunt to the kids, the leader should practice falling on her own to make sure that she knows how to fall. First, you need to be very relaxed. Then let yourself fall forward, not backward, so that you can catch yourself with your hands. Make sure that people don't let their heads or faces touch the ground. Everything should be done on the exhale and with caution.

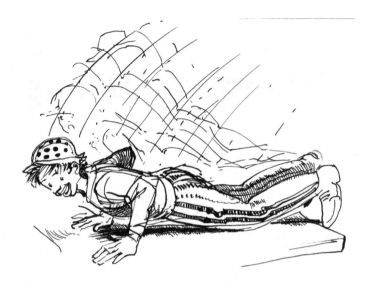

You can also choose to fall in a circular manner by turning in a spiral onto your shoulder as you fall. To start with, use slow instrumental music that emphasizes this effect.

1. *Learn to delay the fall.*

2. *Think about how you are going to fall and at which moment.*

3. *Fall to music that comes to a climax within 30–50 seconds.*

4. *Fall in a relaxed manner.*

5. *Finally, once you have the hang of it, do the fall without mats.*

Falling with Boxes

Props: Gym mats; boxes

Music (optional): Music or drumrolls

Instructions: In this exercise, the clowns include boxes in their falls, letting the empty boxes fly. The best of this type of fall includes some kind of "disaster"—something that looks much worse than it really is. "Oof!" sounds and/or screams can enhance the effect. For best results, encourage the clowns to throw/fling the boxes as high and widely as possible.

Here, too, the leader should practice the exercise first along the length of the gym. A row of gym mats could mark the start of the fall and after 15 feet or so, the clown actually falls down, tossing boxes into the air. After the leader demonstrates, the participants take a turn at the mats, one by one. The leader should have one or two people waiting to collect the boxes after each fall to keep the game moving.

Falling into the Box

Props: A large box from a television or other equipment or a beanbag chair; a gym mat; cymbals or a drum; a drumstick; cushions or something similar

Music (optional): A drumroll; cymbal clashes

Clowns trip and fall anywhere and over anything...sometimes even disappearing into whatever they fell over.

Instructions: A huge box or a pile of cushions may be ideal for this game. Here, again, participants should practice first with gym mats. Afterward everyone can use the props. Let the participants first feel the pile—boxes, cushions, balloons—so that they know how they will fall and what they should watch out for. For little children, using a huge box—one that is taller than they are—is great fun.

Lead the children through a routine like this:

1. *You stagger toward the pile, box, or whatever.*

2. *Make it look as if you are going to fall in but, at the last minute, you catch yourself. You're not going to fall in after all!*

3. *But suddenly, you end up falling in anyway, leaving part of your body sticking out.*

4. *Before falling in, use your voice or body to make sounds that make it all seem much worse than it is. You could make a long drawn-out shriek—as if you are falling down—and add a handclap when you "reach the bottom."*

5. *At the moment when you fall in, there is some kind of noise such as a drumroll or a clash of cymbals.*

6. *Create a way of falling that no one else thought of.*

Tip: Make sure no one goes in headfirst without stretching their hands out in front of them!

The Oversized Coat or Sweater

Props: An oversized coat, sweater, or other piece of clothing

Music: Music appropriate to the routine

A child moving around in a huge coat or sweater can make her steps invisible because no one can see the legs or feet. She can also make herself look bigger or smaller, depending on the illusion you want to create.

Instructions: Bring in an oversized coat or sweater so that the participants can see the idea in action. Sending a photo (by e-mail) to the participants or their parents in advance is another way to get everyone interested.

Create a path or routine for the children to follow once they are in costume. Fit the participants' actions to the clothing available and consider adding music. Moving to music is a lot of fun for the children in the oversized clothing—and it is great fun to watch, too. Draw a path on the floor so that you can see how long the routine takes, fitting it to the music at the same time. This could be a great way to introduce the new circus.

Of course, something has to go wrong when you wear oversized clothes. This is a great opportunity for the children to practice their falls—individually or in pairs. Using music and a good introduction, help them work out a routine. Find a point in the music where something could happen, another point where the action climaxes, and a final point where everything suddenly stops. Let older children work out their own ideas.

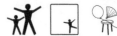

25

A Bucket of Water

Props: A bucket full of confetti, shredded paper, or other materials that can be tossed

Everyone knows that if a clown goes on stage with a bucket of water, something is going to go wrong. There are dozens of versions of tricks clowns can do with buckets of water.

Instructions: Create an act in which one clown taunts another with the bucket. Instead of filling the bucket with water, however, fill it with confetti, shredded paper, or something else. The clowns act as if there is water in the bucket so that it is even more of a surprise when one empties it.

As the leader, you always want to practice this kind of act first. In fact, with younger children, you or an assistant may always want to be the one with the bucket and constantly surprise the group with a new trick. One clown could come running straight at another clown with a bucket, fall over, and get the bucket on his own head. That could be the start of an act for two clowns.

Variation: Let children 8 years old and up make up their own clown act for two clowns; the smart clown and the silly clown might work here. Who will win?

Rope

Props: Rope (or ropes); gym mats (optional)

Instructions: Lay a rope on the floor and let the participants balance along it. You could also draw a line on the floor with chalk, but a rope is more difficult to walk on. Tell the participants that they should imagine that they are walking a tightrope several feet high in the air.

Walking on the high wire is significantly more difficult. Tie a rope across the room, several feet long, so that the participants can walk on it. The highest point should be no more than 3 feet from the ground. Of course you first need to find a suitable rope and make sure that it is secured properly.

Note: Safety is of the utmost importance, and you should be careful when gauging if this game is suitable for your particular situation. Covering the play area with gym mats might make this exercise more safe.

Circus Games for 7–9-Year-Olds

In this age group, the participants will want to think for themselves about what they are going to play. From the age of 8, the children can work together independently to work out a game. Of course, a leader is still necessary because things do not always work. It could be that the game the children created is too long or too short once it is acted out. Or perhaps the children did not understand the instructions.

It is best for an act to have a story line because the participants will still need a clear thread to follow and want to know *why* a certain thing has to be done. Telling children in this age group to put together an act with a rope or a bucket may be too abstract for them. But putting together an act with a bucket or rope that is built around a story or a joke can be worked out much more easily. Giving the game a specific aim is important for the players. Make the story line clear from the start and keep it simple.

Circus Program for 7–9-Year-Olds

There are a large number of interludes—entr'actes—in the games for 7–9-year-olds, which can be combined with the acts, but as was said earlier, they can also be combined with acts for older participants.

The acts with the Hippity Hop Ball or skateboard can be done outside the room or the tent, on a hard surface, or on the street when the circus is about to begin.

Games 33, 36, 37, 45, 46, 47, and 48 in this category are great entr'actes. If, as leader, you are working only with this age group, you can alternate these entr'actes with the acts themselves (e.g., 29, 30, 31, 32, 42, 44, 49). You could create a parade for the acts and do the entr'actes on a separate stage (or in front of the stage).

Here, too, the acts from the program for 4–7-year-olds can also be included and adapted in order to make a more varied program.

Bars

Prop (optional): A ladder; gym mats

Instructions: Many gyms have bars on the wall. If you don't have bars in your gym, then steps or a ladder can be used for this game. Choose a ladder on which you can go up and down on both sides or, in any case, a stepladder that stands up by itself. The participants come up to the ladder and walk up one side and down the other. Put gym mats around the ladder for safety.

When a participant has reached the highest point, the artiste introduces himself with his stage name and tells the audience what he is going to do. Beforehand, ask the participants which act they most want to do in the circus.

Note: Safety is of the utmost importance, and you should be careful when gauging if this game is suitable for your particular situation.

Circus School
Obstacle Course

Props: A collection of objects to use in the obstacle course (boxes, cones, etc.); dress-up clothes; large pieces of material, such as sheets

Instructions: An obstacle course is nothing new for the average gym class, but doing it in costume and makeup is something different. With all of the participants dressed as clowns, an obstacle course offers the children a challenge. They will have fun staging all sorts of pile-ups around the different objects.

Tip: Arrange the gym as a circus school for several weeks so that the participants get used to the atmosphere before the actual performances. Pull stools in a square around the obstacle-course objects and hang large pieces of material to change the space. For a few weeks, everyone can rehearse their acts in this environment.

Two Ladders
and a Bench

Props: Ladders; a bench

Instructions: Gym benches can be arranged across two ladders in such a way that they anchor themselves. Attach the benches so that someone walking across one will feel secure; they should feel confident that the bench will not slip. Make sure you use stepladders that stand up by themselves. Smaller benches also can be used for this purpose. Make sure that the benches don't have splinters.

Give each participant an umbrella to help him keep his balance. To make the act more difficult, invite two people up on the bench. Extra possibilities: Include a hoop that participants have to go through. Have the children walk backward, stand on one leg, etc. Children ages 8 and up can form pairs and create their own acts.

Note: Safety is of the utmost importance, and you should be careful when gauging if this game is suitable for your particular situation.

Hippity Hop Ball

Props: A Hippity Hop Ball (a huge ball, big enough to sit on, with a loop that riders hold onto), preferably several; a stopwatch

Instructions: In an event such as a circus or an obstacle race, a Hippity Hop Ball is great fun. Have the children try out things to do with the ball apart from bouncing. A true artiste can do things with an object such as a Hippity Hop Ball that no one else ever thought of doing.

Ask:

- *How long can you stay in balance on the Hippity Hop Ball?*
- *Who can stay on more than a minute without falling off?*
- *Who can do the most original trick?*

Make sure you have a stopwatch to time the participants. Give everyone a turn so they can see what they can do. Then start brainstorming to see what the group can imagine. Suggestions might include: bounce holding on with one hand, bounce high, bounce low, bounce forward or backward, bounce in circles, etc.

Skateboard

Prop: A skateboard

Note: Use outdoor space if possible.

The skateboard has appeared in modern dance theater, as happens with the more interesting playthings. Certainly it won't be long before it also appears in the circus.

Instructions: Tell the children that a skateboard cannot be used indoors, so they will have to create stunts to perform outdoors. Real skateboarders jump over obstacles with their boards, fly from a slope, and land on a lower level.

Invite participants to come up with simpler tricks such as having two people on the board, having one person sitting or lying down on the board (while someone else pushes), and striking a pose. There are plenty of ideas to try out with a skateboard. In the circus performance, the skaters can play to the crowds on the streets. This is a good way to include this group in the performance—or during the intermission, when some people leave the "tent" for a short break.

Note: Safety is of the utmost importance, and you should be careful when gauging if this game is suitable for your particular situation.

A Ball, a Book, and a Tray

Props: Various objects

Music: Music appropriate to the routine

Instructions: Here is another game for the balance beam. This is made for those who want to be more adventurous. Give each participant three objects, pile them on top of each other, and then have the children try to move without dropping any of them.

This game is most fun when players use three really different objects such as a book, a tray, and a ball. Be sure to choose objects that cannot break or hurt anyone if they fall. You could also include the obstacle course and ask players to do a circuit carrying these objects.

pairs

Cook with Pans

Props: A set of old pans; a chef's hat; a white apron

Instructions: Participants may know the Swedish Chef from the Muppet films. He is a quirky character, who speaks a strange language, and who is always trying to prepare some dish. Unfortunately nothing he tries goes right. In the circus, there should also be an act that makes no sense and achieves absolutely nothing. That could well be the Swedish Chef. He is always bringing in pans full of things that have nothing whatever to do with cooking. The chef juggles with things that he puts into or takes out of the pan. He might put in or pull out a rubber chicken, an iron, a comb with strands of spaghetti in it, a dictionary, a glasses case, etc.

Ask the participants: *Who can make up a good story about the Swedish Chef? What will he cook, and what will he call this unique dish? What kind of gibberish does he speak?*

The chef is just an example. You can create completely different characters for the entr'acte as long as this act does what it is meant to do: put some space between two different circus acts. For instance, perhaps your entr'acte revolves around someone who keeps popping up in a diver's suit and trying to dive into a bucket.

Try pairing participants and have them create an entr'acte.

Decoration

Props: Decorative objects and material

Instructions: Decorating a space is a special skill. The space where the acts will be performed can easily be decorated with cut-out stencils of stars, shiny balls, party lights, Christmas lights, large pieces of material, paper decorations, etc. Assign a special group to this task so that you, as the leader, can concentrate on the acts. In any given class, there will always be some people who are not interested in the performance side or who have some physical obstacle to joining in. Make a timetable for your decorating group so they know when each item needs to be ready.

Fantasy Circus

Props: Drawing and crafts material

Instructions: Ask the participants to draw or build a model of their fantasy circus. Try drawing or making a model yourself as inspiration. Designing a circus can be a relaxing period between the other circus rehearsals, and it can result in more creativity and involvement. Let the participants explain all the things that can happen in their fantasy circuses. Getting the children to talk about their circus models can give you insight into the way children's fantasy worlds function and open your group to the circus's many possibilities.

The Broom

Props: Brooms, preferably soft and lightweight

Instructions: A soft broom that is easy to use can inspire an act. A long broom has two possibilities for play: the handle and the broom head. Participants—dressed as clowns—can use the handle to hold someone back or to poke or touch them. The broom head can be used to sweep someone off her feet or sweep away something important.

Divide the class into pairs of children to work out an act, dance, or other imaginative use of the broom. The youngest players may need your help (or that of an assistant) to come up with a story or joke and a sequence to illustrate it. Older players will want to think of something for themselves and get busy. Give pairs time to work through their ideas and then have each pair present their act to the group.

Example: Players energetically sweep at a piece of dirt that won't go away... because it is painted on the floor. This idea can be a nice start for an act where patience soon wears thin, someone gets blamed, and everyone involved ends up getting poked with the broom handle.

Tip: A broom can also be dangerous, so its use in the act must be rehearsed. Have players practice first using cardboard tubes or something made of plastic.

Elastic

Props: Large elastic bands

At a hardware store, you can find strong elastic bands. Some pieces of elastic are so big and strong that a person can swing from them. Call a local business and ask if it sells something along the lines of strong bungee cords about 3 feet long.

With a partner, you can hang from the elastic and make all kinds of funny movements. One partner stands still with the elastic around his middle and the other puts the elastic around her middle and—carefully—stretches away from her partner.

Variation: Many children have at some time played with a Chinese jump rope. In this game, two children stand with the elastic around their ankles in a particular pattern. A third person jumps the rope, completing a specific set of moves within that pattern (e.g., both feet in the middle, both feet on the out-side, left foot in and right foot out, right foot in and left foot out). Who can complete the most moves in succession?

Note: Safety is of the utmost importance, and you should be careful when gauging if this game is suitable for your particular situation.

What Job?

Props: A blackboard or whiteboard; chalk or pens

Instructions: The circus includes many different jobs. Make a list of as many different circus jobs as you can think of on the board. Briefly talk about each job—from clown to horse trainer—and ask the class about the tools and equipment that people in those jobs use, what the people look like, and how they behave.

Divide the group into pairs. Have each pair choose a job and rehearse a depiction of it—without speaking. They should create a mini-performance to illustrate the job, lasting just one minute. The rest of the group can decide whether all the elements of the job have been covered.

Circus Pelmanism

Props: Cardboard; scissors; pens; pictures of circus performers; list of phrases related to the circus

Instructions: The game of Pelmanism (also known as Concentration) involves remembering the location of pairs of cards. With a group of children, make a number of cards with circus jobs and phrases drawn or written on them. Each card should be part of a pair of matching cards. Lay the cards face down and let each child turn over one card at a time. When a player turns a card, he then tries to find its match. Maybe someone turned it over before, and he can remember where it is. If not, the player makes a wild guess. If a player finds the pair, he wins a set. Who can find the most pairs? If the group is not yet familiar with the circus, this can be a good way to start.

Clowniness

Props: Red clown noses

Instructions: A clown can make all kinds of faces and express dozens of emotions. In this game, players take turns portraying one of those emotions, and the rest of the group tries to guess what that emotion is.

For this game, the leader has a single attribute to give the clown form. It could be a red nose, a silly orange wig, or an oversize coat. It should give a child the feeling that just for a moment she is really a clown.

The children sit in a circle; the leader gives the nose (or wig) to someone. The child puts on the nose and acts out an emotion that a clown might have—perhaps he laughs. This is done without speaking or making other sounds (though that could be a variation on the game). Whoever guesses the emotion wins the round. He or she then puts on the nose and shows another emotion. After the group has practiced the game a few different times, you will notice that the children start to think of more and more emotions. It may help to draw the emotions or to watch a film of a clown before you begin.

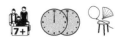

What Does the Clown Look Like?

Props: Pictures of clowns; drawing materials; a computer

Instructions: Over the past one hundred years, clowns have taken many different forms. A clown from one circus was not allowed to look anything like the clowns working for the competition! Each clown worked at having his own particular appearance.

To give the children an idea of the variety of clowns, bring in some pictures of different clowns (e.g., pictures of Auguste and Whiteface clowns as well as clowns from the Italian Comedia dell'Arte). You can find these in library books or by Googling *clowns + pictures* on the Internet. Let each participant develop his own clown style—both costume and makeup—using ideas from the pictures. Make a competition out of it—with a prize, of course!—and let the children demonstrate their styles. On a nice day you can hold a parade outside with all the clowns.

Talking Clown!

Instructions: A clown can speak many languages, of course. He can also understand—or misunderstand—other people with all the repercussions that that brings with it. Tell the children to imagine themselves as clowns who speak in a made-up language called Jabber talk. It isn't a real language; it is just whatever the players make of it. Show the group what you mean by demonstrating your own made-up language.

Have pairs of children hold a conversation in which both speak a different language. Which children can converse the longest and manage to convey a "real" message to each other?

As preparation, you might want to discuss a theme in normal speech. Pairs of children can then try repeating this discussion using jabber talk. After that they might try coming up with their own themes for discussion.

Tip: You might suggest that the players use special letters or vowels more often.

Anxiety

Instructions: Suggest to the children that a clown can suddenly get frightened by something that no one else is afraid of—a baby mouse, for instance. Or maybe he is suddenly afraid of heights. No matter what the situation, a clown is very good at exaggerating his or her feelings.

Ask the children: *What could a clown be afraid of?*

Let the group form pairs and imagine situations that they then rehearse. Eventually each pair will perform for the group. If necessary, give the players some examples:

- a clown that is afraid of a wind-up mouse that whizzes across the floor
- a clown that is afraid of a talking doll
- a clown that is afraid of sneezes—and suddenly has to sneeze

Snake Charmer

Props: Nylon cord; a rubber snake; basket; a flute/recorder; a cloth; costumes for the snake charmer and the assistant; a CD player

Music: Eastern flute music that the charmer "plays"

Instructions: Some circus acts seem to be all-time favorites. Among these is the snake charmer's act. You may want to include this act in your lineup. After you select a snake charmer, prepare the props. Tie a rubber snake by a very long nylon cord to a hook in the ceiling. When the act begins, the basket sits alone on the stage. Then the snake charmer comes on stage with his flute. The charmer removes the cover (or a cloth) from the top of the basket and begins to "play" his flute. Somewhere offstage, an unseen assistant gently pulls on the cord, and the snake rises from the basket. The snake could look very real—or ridiculously unreal!

Tip: The act works best if the audience can't see the assistant.

Rope Trick

Props: Paper; drawing materials; props for the acts; DVD of Tommy Cooper (optional)

Instructions: Begin by talking about—or showing a DVD of—magician and comedian Tommy Cooper. In Cooper's act—in between the highlights— the tricks always went wrong. For instance, making a rope stand up straight is a well-known trick. After doing this feat, Cooper would show the audience that there was a stick hidden in the rope.

Magicians can buy all sorts of tricks and props in party stores; some are cheap and others more expensive. But tell the children they also can develop props for themselves. Talk with them, for example, about making a suitcase with a hidden compartment or a "rock" made out of papier-mâché. Have the participants make sketches of their act and the props they will need. Then— with help—they can make the props they need.

The Trick
That Went Wrong

Instructions: The trick that goes wrong is often more fun than one that works. The key is in the timing, humor, and material—and someone who can bungle the trick convincingly. Think, for instance, of a knife-throwing trick that goes wrong but (fortunately) uses a retractable blade of soft plastic or rubber knives that miss the board with someone standing in front of it. You will find that many families have some of these "joke" items that they would be willing to loan to your group. Explain and demonstrate one or two items to get the children thinking. Then divide the class into smaller groups and give each group time to imagine and prepare an act.

Play the Musician!

Props: (Fake) musical instruments

Music: Music appropriate to the routine

Instructions: Once an act is finished, the stage has to be rearranged and props have to be replaced. Between the acts, have a fake orchestra—the marching orchestra—entertain. This "orchestra" doesn't need to know how to play music, and the instruments don't need to be real. The accordion player who has a CD player built into his "instrument" can act as if he is really playing; other artistes can mime to music played on CD.

Rehearse the orchestra to make sure that no one realizes that this is not a real orchestra. Play the musician!

My Eyebrows Go in Two Directions

Instructions: Ask the children to think of people who can do tricks with their faces that other people cannot do. Some people can wiggle their ears, fold their tongues over, or move their eyebrows separately. Every circus should have someone who can do "something." Very often a class has a number of people with such talents. Ask for volunteers and let the children show off for everyone. For the final performance, you might even invite people from the audience to show off the special tricks that they can do with their bodies.

My Rabbit Can Dance!

Props: A circus pet

Instructions: A real circus has animals—especially a children's circus! Ask the children if they know anyone who has a pet that can perform tricks. You will be amazed by the things people teach animals to do: a parrot who talks, a cat who goes for walks, a rabbit who can dance, a pony who lies down and stands up again.

With even two animal acts, you can make your lineup even more interesting. But remember: Animals won't always perform their tricks when there is a large audience. But, as the leader, you can warn the performers about this. Prepare the performer to adapt the act if need be. For example, the performer calls out, "And now the pony who won't lie down," preparing for the worst. If by chance the pony does lie down, it is a great opportunity for acting utterly astonished...and the audience will love it.

Hula Hoops

Props: Hula hoops

Music: Music appropriate to the routine

Instructions: Hula hoops, like marbles, can suddenly be "in" and then go out of fashion for years. Ask who has a hula hoop at home. Try to get as many as possible. As with all the acts, let the participants choose which props they are interested in and what they want to work on. Circus performers have their own preferences; you can't ask a trapeze artist to be a horse trainer. Let the children practice to see how long they can keep the hoop from falling to the floor. Are they able to do it only around their waists or are some children able to keep the hoop turning around more difficult places such as the arm? Try two people in one hoop.

An act should always be built from the simple to the more difficult, and an assistant can encourage the audience to applaud when something works right. Participants start with one hoop and add more, one by one. The more hoops a performer can keep spinning, the more people will applaud. Use music that begins calmly and builds, getting faster or more exciting.

The **Lions** and the **Lion Tamer**

Props: A circus ring; lion costumes; a lion tamer's costume with moustache; a whip; lighting that can be dimmed

Music: Music appropriate to the routine

Instructions: You can't use real lions in this lion tamer's act, but those children dressed in lion suits move just like lions—and can they roar! The lions can jump, put their forepaws in the air, and even jump over each other.

Make sure you have the lights dimmed so that the lions look more real. Practice with the "lions" how to walk slowly on hands and feet at the same time, as elegantly as real lions. The lions also need to be trained to jump over each other. Show them how to lash out at the lion tamer for extra effect! (You could use a CD of real lions roaring as music here.) The lion tamer needs to believe in what he's doing, and this should show. He has to create an act that oozes authority, snapping his whip over and over.

In costume shops, you can buy animal masks for very little, and perhaps a few mothers can buy the material to make thick lion suits. Participants might prefer to wear a ballet suit—black stretch—and simply add feet, claws, a tail, and a mask. It would be simpler and leave them with more freedom of movement.

As leader, plan exactly how this act should look—the entrance, how the lions will walk in the ring, and the sequence of the tricks. Otherwise it won't look believable. A flourishing exit, perhaps via a trampoline that is partly hidden at the side, can create a wonderful spectacle.

Which Animal?

Use this game for warming-up or closing down the class.

Instructions: This game can be helpful with a group of children who do not know each other well yet. Make a ring of chairs; use one more chair than you have participants. The person sitting to the left of the empty chair says, "I want...to come and sit next to me." The named person says, "What animal should I be?" The first child names an animal, and the second comes across the circle behaving like that animal. He or she can also make appropriate sounds.

The Last Dodo

Props: A stuffed animal to portray the "last of its breed"; drawing materials

Instructions: The last dodo died in Mauritius more than three hundred years ago. A few bones and drawings can teach us what the bird looked like and how it moved. It doesn't seem to have been able to fly, and that was one reason why it died out.

A circus should have some kind of rare animal performing. It can be introduced with the explanation that "the director discovered this animal just the day before yesterday and bought it at an auction." The dodo is just an example. The children can even make up a "never-before-seen" animal to include. Maybe it makes strange noises. Can it do tricks?

How do the handlers bring the animal in? Is it walking, in a cart, on a platform, or under a sheet? Remember that in the circus everything is exaggerated and blown out of proportion. The audience is about to see a very rare animal indeed!

An animal like this is fun only if the handler or ringmaster has amazing things to say about it. These might include the animal's Latin name, its height and length, how many eggs it lays, etc. He or she should also explain how it was captured. Draw the animal or make trick photos. Project the photos either in advance to make the audience curious or when the act begins.

Circus Games for 9–10-Year-Olds

Around the age of 9, children let go of the fantasy world—at least if their development goes according to what is considered "average." Of course every child is different, and as the leader you will want to remember that.

A 9-year-old is also more able to express himself verbally and will give an opinion about the subject in question. Physically he is growing into a more grown-up child; he can also take more physical strain. In terms of the circus, this means that he can do gymnastics, sports, and endurance exercises.

The acts in this section are more logical, and the subjects are chosen specially to back this up. A clown can sometimes do really silly things, and this may entertain some people. But people recognize that it is silly behavior! By this age, too, children can learn their lines by heart and make presentations in the circus.

The sensory development of children has advanced by this time, and the children are more able to anticipate danger. This means that they also may take more risks, so caution is required if participants want to try dangerous balancing acts. After all, these are still children needing guidance through the new circus exercises.

Circus Program for 9–10-Year-Olds

Below is a list of acts well suited to a performance by this age group. The ringmaster can announce a lineup of some of the following acts:

1. Game 63: Stilt Walkers
2. Game 55: Duo Shoes
3. Game 61: The Woman with Three Arms
4. Game 57: Bed of Nails
5. Game 58: Sword Swallower
6. Game 69: The Ball Throwers of Lutjebrook
7. Game 64: Marching Band
8. Game 59: The Flipper Dancers
9. Game 60: Appia and Tonio Stronzo, the Weight-Lifting Brothers
10. Game 65: Bike-Bell Orchestra (entr'acte)
11. Game 56: Chimps!
12. Game 70: The Red Men (entr'acte)
13. Game 67: The Ring Throwers from Bombay (finale)

Naturally, acts from another age-group category can be adapted and used in the circus for 9–10-year-olds.

One-Man Circus

Props: Drawing and crafts materials; heavy cloths or a tent to create an enclosed space

Music: Circus-type music (see the Resources section at the back of the book for some recommendations)

Everyone is accustomed to going to the circus in a big-top tent. What does a mini-circus look like? This game will show you.

Instructions: People from the audience are invited to a mini-circus. They must first pass through a larger space, walk down a hallway, and then come to a much smaller space. The louder the circus music becomes, the smaller the space the people go through. Finally they come to a one-person tent set in a small space such as a corner.

There is just a single chair there, and it is as if the visitor is looking at a mini-circus, like a kind of tiny peepshow. A curtain hangs by the opening, and visitors can see puppets moving inside. Someone is working them from behind—playing all the circus personalities through the puppets—but the visitor can't see who it is.

Each mini-circus performance lasts just two minutes. A visitor is welcome to watch the whole show or watch for just a short time and then go out again. Then the next visitor can approach the entrance. This game, and the setting that goes with it, should be visited only between performances. And the visit to this little space should be surrounded with all kinds of mystery. Often this mini-show makes an even greater impact than the other circus.

Duo Shoes

Props: Old shoes in big sizes (make sure it is okay to cut these up); tools for working on the shoes; strong glue; rope; pieces of leather

Instructions: It is not only clowns who carry strange objects—such as an extra long pole—around with them. These days, trapeze artists and acrobats festoon themselves in fancy costumes and accessories.

This is an example of an act that can make the circus more interesting. A pair of children comes on stage wearing shoes that are joined at the toes. Each "shoe" has two heels—one at either end—but the toes are glued together so that two performers can walk in them at the same time. Of course, you could simply bind the children's feet together, but if you can get old shoes from an adult, you can cut holes at the toes and fasten the two shoes together at that point. You could stick another strip of leather over the joint so that you don't see the open toes.

It may be simpler to make a shoe with one toe and two heels out of cardboard. You can even paint this to look like a shoe: simply cover it with dark shoe polish and let it dry. The polish will make it hard as well. If you want, you can then spray it with hairspray to fix the color.

For another pair of performers, make a coat or hat that two people can wear at the same time. Invite pairs of children to come up with an extra-special prop of this kind. When the prop is made, have the pair work out how to move together to the music.

Chimps!

Instructions: Start by holding a discussion about who has been to a circus and seen animals there. Ask the children:

- *What animals did you see?*
- *What kind of tricks did the animals do?*
- *Were there chimps?*

This is a game to play in pairs—pairs of chimps. What do chimps do? They mimic people; they pick fleas off of each other; they jump and throw things. They scream at people.

Have everyone gather in a circle. To start the game, demonstrate a few chimp movements and yells. Then ask everyone in the circle to do a chimp trick that is mimicked by all the other children.

Each pair then thinks up an act of about one minute in length. The act must include a jump, a yell, a flea-picking movement, a stumbling/walking movement. For the presentation in the circus, a pair should be chosen through a public "audition." These chimps should also have costumes.

Bed of Nails

Props: A bed of nails; a fakir's costume

Instructions: The fakir lying on a bed of nails is another act the audience will enjoy. You cannot, of course, let a child lie on a real bed of nails. But from the audience's point of view, the scene has to look real!

Use real nails at the front and sides of the bed. For the rest of the bed, use nails made of cardboard, foam, or polystyrene. If necessary, drill holes to hold these "nails" so that they stay put. A parent could help make this prop.

Construct the bed on wheels; then it can be rolled in and out before the audience can look too closely and realize that it is not real. Paint can cover up many things, and a cloth covering everything but the side that can be felt by the public will make them believe that it is real.

The fakir who lies or sits on this bed should be chosen carefully: He really has to look like a fakir. Here again, a costume that shines and twinkles will add to the illusion and enhance the act.

Sword Swallower

Props: Fake knives and a couple of real ones; music; a table with a nice cloth to put things on; a beautifully costumed assistant; a shiny suit for the sword swallower with fake bracelets, etc.

Tip: You can find retractable knives in party shops.

Important Note: With all the games in this book the absolute priority has to be the safety of the participants and the audience. There should not be a single moment where anyone is in danger. For all the games the first rule is: Test it yourself first to be sure that it works. Also, be sure to check in advance if real knives are permitted in your school or by your organization.

Instructions: A good arts-and-crafts teacher will be able to make paper or cardboard knives that retract but still look real. The sword swallower himself should also look a little bit dangerous; a well-costumed character will ensure that the public is more concerned with the person brandishing those knives than his act. A black eye patch, a few painted "scars," an open shirt with a fake tattoo—it all helps create an atmosphere.

The sword swallower has a table where he—and you—can switch real knives for fakes at the very last minute—but not before he has slashed an apple in half in front of the audience with a real knife! As he turns around, he can put down the real knife and pick up the fake knife, which he then pretends to "swallow" to the hilt.

The sword swallower should work to the swell of the music for extra effect. The assistant should look completely unconcerned at first and then, suddenly, exaggeratedly anxious just as the moment approaches. A drumroll at this point can help as well. All of this is meant to distract the audience. A presenter or ringmaster can also draw the audience's attention. And you could always have a clown wander in and fall over... so that it seems as if the sword swallower has lost his concentration. Great drama!

Prepare the act carefully. Make sure the assistant, the props, and the music are all in place before the artiste, himself, appears.

Note: Safety is of the utmost importance, and you should be careful when gauging if this game is suitable for your particular situation.

The Flipper Dancers

Props: Ballet clothes; flippers with matching (colored) snorkel and mask

Music: Music appropriate to the routine

Instructions: Different colored flippers, masks, and snorkels already make an eye-catching impression. The children can put on the flippers and masks with their ballet clothes and invent a dance. It is hard work to walk in flippers, but if they do it all at the same time in a chorus line it is always fun. Choreograph a flipper-ballet.

Or have the children put the flippers on their hands and create a monster with lots of arms by standing one behind the other. A parade of the flipper dancers through the arena can be hilarious!

Appia and Tonio Stronzo, the Weight-Lifting Brothers

Props: Painted poles with weights (painted buckets)

Instructions: The Stronzo brothers are fierce-looking characters. They have huge moustaches and maybe beards; they are quite round and wear old-fashioned muscle-man swimsuits. They pick up poles that are painted to look as if they're made of metal. The "weights" on either end of the poles also look very heavy, but they're plastic buckets with "150 pounds" painted on each side. You also could use papier-mâché balls painted black.

Various other weights are strewn around or piled in a cart. If you use music or the recorded cheering of fans, the act can be made even more exciting. The Stronzo brothers should do lots of grunting and groaning when they lift the weights.

The Woman
with Three Arms

Props: Materials for designing an extraordinary person (papier-mâché, paint, clothes, latex, etc.)

Instructions: The famous Barnum & Bailey Circus, an American show from the early twentieth century, always had extraordinary characters to be seen. Often these were people with some physical abnormality. Of course, the abnormality was not always genuine. But highlighting the appearance of an "extraordinary person"—someone with three arms, for instance—is definitely a way of drawing in the public.

Make an arm out of papier-mâché. Paint it and attach it inside an adapted shirt. Maybe you could even borrow a false arm from a hospital. Other ideas:

- a Pinocchio-type character with a very long nose (the nose can be put on by a makeup artist)

- two children in one suit to give the appearance of a person with more than two arms

- someone with a long tail that moves

- In costume shops, you can buy latex masks that can give your face or other body parts a very strange look. If you attach anything with glue, make sure you also buy the product to remove it afterward. You might also see if anyone knows someone who is good with makeup and would be willing to add some peculiarities with suitable materials.

- Write a speech that the ringmaster can use to introduce this strange creature.

Tip: Have the class first make drawings of what their extraordinary person is going to look like.

The **Ringmaster**

Props: A microphone and sound system; pen and paper; various props for the ringmaster (a walking stick or baton, for instance); a tailcoat

Instructions: Children love to play the ringmaster. A ringmaster has to command attention with his appearance and perhaps with his size. A ringmaster also needs to have a big voice so that he can announce the artistes loudly and dramatically. That is an art in itself.

Form pairs to write a speech for the ringmaster. It should be two minutes in length. The ringmaster finishes his act with an introduction of the first act. Each pair rehearses this and, after 25 minutes, they do it for the group. Who can look the biggest, speak loudest, and make the biggest impression?

Stilt Walkers

Props: Stilts and extra-long clothing

Music (optional): Slow classical music

Instructions: Walking on stilts, wearing extra long clothes, and announcing the arrival of the circus is a very special act. For many centuries and in many countries, stilt walkers have walked the streets, showing off their skills or getting publicity for one event or another.

Find out who has stilts at home and who can actually use them! If you are performing outside, it is important to make sure that slow stilt walking is accompanied by slow classical music.

Letting stilt walkers work together is an art in itself. Practice well as this is a very individual matter and accidents can happen if participants don't work out in advance who is going to walk where. Stilt walkers often know many tricks to do on stilts. For instance, they know how to stand still in a crowd—or give the impression that they are standing still—and they can walk as slowly as a giraffe. Masks might further emphasize the mystery of the stilt walker. On the other hand, masks limit the wearer's vision.

Notes:

- Stilt walkers should be accompanied by you or an assistant when they are performing.
- Safety is of the utmost importance, and you should be careful when gauging if this game is suitable for your particular situation.

Marching Band

Props: Instruments that musicians can fasten to their bodies

Instructions: In the circus, the band often sits above the entrance where everyone walks into the ring. Consider using a real marching band between acts. A marching band could consist of a drummer, a brass section, a few percussionists, and some flautists.

Some of the group could carry things that make a sound when they walk, such as bells, triangles, tambourines, wood blocks, cymbals, bongos, etc. The important thing is to agree on a rhythm or a beat that forms the basis of the "band."

If you can work together with a local music school, you will immediately ensure a larger audience. The supporters of the musicians will bring their families along!

Bike-Bell Orchestra

Props: Anything that makes a sound

Instructions: A marching band can have members who use things that make a sound but don't seem to be musical instruments. Consider, for example, hitting a watering can with a stick to keep the rhythm.

Ask the children to imagine a group of musicians who have only broom handles and their hands with which to make music. The sound of this band would be very different. With each act, have the children come up with new "instruments" where the hands remain the basic rhythm keepers: broomsticks, pans, pan lids, wooden planks, bicycle bells, etc.

The Conductor

Props: A conductor's suit and baton

The circus has plenty of characters and roles. Small children do not yet know all of the roles people play in the circus.

Instructions: Begin this game by naming all the different circus jobs the class can think of. Write them on a board. Assuming someone names the orchestra conductor, focus on this role. Every orchestra needs a conductor—even the circus orchestra. Apart from keeping time and rhythm, the conductor has to be showy enough to lead the show around the ring and off again.

Have the children imagine themselves as the conductor. Ask each participant to think up a special walk for his or her conductor. Then ask various conductors to demonstrate. Is there someone who can lead and still be funny? Have the group pick a favorite conductor. Ask him or her to rehearse to a piece of music and see if the routine has enough conducting gestures to "support" the music.

The Ring Throwers from Bombay

Props: A conductor's suit and baton

When people see that some of the circus artistes come from faraway places, they really want to see the act. The ring throwers come from Bombay—a place that probably few people in the class have visited. The ring throwers are, of course, world famous in Bombay, and their fame has spread ahead of them.

Instructions: Participants can use almost anything to juggle: balls, clubs, rings, etc. The idea is to throw these objects into the air, pass them from one hand to another, and catch the first one. There is a pattern to it. Otherwise a juggler could throw everything into the air at once and the game would be over because everything would just fall to the ground.

Tell the children that they need to get to know each object before they can juggle with it. Ask them: *Watch how it behaves as you toss it upward. Does it fall right away? Does it twist or turn in the air?* Explain that they should adapt their juggling pattern based on the way the objects behave.

When using the rings, begin with one, add another, and another, and another. The ring throwers from Bombay have one catcher and the rest of the group throws rings to him fast, one after the other. The throwers stand in a semicircle.

Split the class into several smaller groups so they can all practice at the same time. In each group, the throwers and catcher should eventually switch places. Which group is best at this game? Make sure that no one gets hurt with the rings. Keep an eye on the speed with which the children are throwing. Begin slowly and let them build speed gradually.

Circus Balls

Props: Small balls (possibly homemade)

Instructions: Throwing a ball into the air with your hand is one of the first activities that a person learns to do. Have everyone stand in a circle or spread out around the room. On your signal, everyone starts throwing and catching.

Have the children try throwing the ball with the other hand. Tell them to catch the ball in the same hand with which they are throwing it. This won't be easy for everyone. Next, have them try throwing with one hand and catching with the other.

Throw two balls: Have the children take a ball in each hand; throw two balls and catch with two hands: the ball they throw with the right hand should be the ball they catch with the right hand, etc.

Now have participants throw two balls with one hand, one after the other, and catch them in one hand. They then throw the ball in an arc from one hand to the other, throwing up ball number 2 just before catching ball number 1. The children can create more difficult combinations as their skills increase.

Who will become the famous ball throwers of Lutjebroek?

The Ball Throwers of Lutjebroek

Props: Small balls; costumes

Instructions: Direct the children to use three balls now, always throwing the next ball into the lineup just under the other one. Remind the children to arc the throw as practiced in the previous game. It is all a matter of timing. The ball throwers of Lutjebroek can do all sorts of tricks other than this standard one, which many people already know.

Have the children change places if they are throwing balls to each other and agree on a sequence and a count. Otherwise it will be chaotic. First they should make a sketch of the group on paper. Then they will want to pace it out in the ring, as they have to know exactly where everyone should stand to start off.

They should practice the routine "dry" to make sure that everyone can re-member the sequence of movements and the count. They can practice switching places when they are able to throw several balls to each other.

This group of ball throwers should, naturally, have special costumes so that people can see that they come from some far-off place. They should have a very individual style of clothes, with interestingly colored shorts or pants that contrast with the colors of the balls.

The Red Men

Props: Red plastic caps; red makeup; red clothing; props to play with, such as balls, rings, stuffed animals, or boxes to toss or move

Music: Music appropriate to the routine

Instructions: The Blue Man Group performs all over the world. These male performers wear blue makeup, are made "bald" by wearing a latex mask over the head, and have an act in which they do not speak but are constantly in awe of everything they see and touch. It is an act that grew out of vaudeville where you used to see acts of this sort.

An old plastic ball serves well to make a bald head if you cut it in half, but something simpler like trimming a plastic shopping bag could also work. Have participants paint the cap red and pull it tight over their hair (remind children of the dangers of suffocation) when it is dry. The children can put red makeup on their faces and dress entirely in red.

The group—anywhere from three to ten people—enters to the music. Make sure there are props suitable for mime and see that they suit the music. Have the children think up some things the group can do with the props once they are in the ring. Encourage them to imagine ways to use the props that the audience would not expect.

Example: The balls they throw in the air turn out to be painted hard-boiled eggs that the participants eat after peeling off the shells.

Circus Games for 10–12-Year-Olds

A 10-year-old becomes aware of the fact that she is growing up. She also realizes that it won't be too long before she leaves grade school. At this age, the children's bodies are growing; their minds can manage a greater degree of abstraction and are ready for more difficult work.

All of this is a benefit to the performance of circus games. An older child will see a game as a challenge—and he will tackle that challenge until he has it under his belt. Speed, timing, daring, doing several things at the same time, cooperation, discovering new material, intelligence—all of these things are characteristics of this age group. You will be able to let the participants write the presenter's texts and even plan acts that need a plot. Once you have explained the assignment to them, they will be able to work on it for themselves.

Exercises for strength are also possible for this age group. The balancing exercises described earlier in the book and the juggling exercises can all be intensified with this age group.

Circus Program for 10–12-Year-Olds

Which acts best lend themselves to a performance by this age group? This category includes many numbers that can grow into an act. A suggested lineup for the ringmaster to announce includes the following acts:

1. Game 75: Rolling Plank
2. Game 73: The Men in Black
3. Game 82: Clowns and Music (entr'acte)
4. Game 81: Pyramid for Six
5. Game 77: Three Ladders
6. Game 83: The Limbo (entr'acte)
7. Game 78: Scooter or Tricycle?
8. Game 84: Trampoline (entr'acte)
9. Game 79: Bike Act
10. Game 87: Walking Money (entr'acte)
11. Game 88: Thimble (entr'acte)
12. Game 80: Roller Skates
13. Game 89: Ball and Cloth (entr'acte)
14. Game 96: Cossack Dance
15. Game 90: Three Cigar Boxes (entr'acte)
16. Game 92: Frisbee Throwers
17. Game 93: The Beach-Ball Slammers
18. Game 98: Playback Show
19. Game 99: Ribbon Dancers (entr'acte)
20. Game 100: Chinese Plates
21. Game 95: Shadowy Dreams (finale)

Grandpa's Circus

Props: A collection of odd objects; paper; writing materials

Instructions: The Lost Property office at the circus has saved your grandfather's circus props. You are the grandchild, inheriting his personal effects 50 years later. It is up to you to breathe life back into them. Tell the stories of these objects to bring them back to life.

Example: A rolling pin. "My grandfather was a clown and in one of his acts he had to crush cake sprinkles under a cloth using the rolling pin. What he didn't know was that his partner had put something else under the cloth as well as sprinkles. Usually it was something like an egg...or several eggs...."

What are all the things in this collection? Some of the things seem to have nothing at all to do with the circus, like that rolling pin, a lawnmower, a bike wheel, a purse. Participants explain to the public what grandpa did with all these things and what kind of acts they did in his circus 50 years ago. This act can include several grandchildren who each choose one object and write a story about it.

The Exhibition

Props: Curtains; display materials, such as photos (which can be staged), clown noses made of papier-mâché, masks, costumes for the trapeze artist

Instructions: Make an exhibition of circus props. Set up tables where the exhibition can stay for a week, establishing the circus atmosphere. Hang heavy cloths like in the theater—preferably old red velvet curtains—behind the tables. Who will open the exhibition? Invite someone who can give a speech about life in the circus.

The Men in Black

Props: Black clothes; black masks; black gloves; music; props to fit the routine

Instructions: The men in black originated in the Black Theater in Prague. In this act, the performers dress in black, with their hands in black gloves and their faces completely hidden by black masks. The space where the audience sits is completely blacked out. This allows the men in black to move about without being seen. Only the objects they carry in their hands can be seen. Of course this needs some skillful lighting.

You could also build a replica of the Black Theater of Prague in the classroom: Create a dark space by pushing several partitions together. Close the curtains, but pin back one of them so that the public can look into this black box. The men in black can enter from the sides with their objects and glide around the space to music.

Grab the Cloth

Props: A colored cloth for each player—around 12 × 12 inches

Instructions: In unison, participants throw a cloth in the air and catch it again. A piece of cloth is not very easy to control, so it is a good idea to experiment with different types of material to see what works best. Cut out as many pieces as you need and hem them on the sewing machine so they do not fray.

Ask the children to stand in a line. On the count of three, everyone throws his cloth into the air and catches it again.

Variation: Each player takes one step to the right and catches the cloth of his neighbor. The person who sees there is no cloth when she steps to the right quickly runs round and joins the other end of the line and catches the cloth of the first player who stepped to the right. This game requires skill and dexterity, but it can be great fun and excellent for enhancing teamwork.

Rolling Plank

Props: PVC tubing around 4–6 inches in diameter and a maximum of 12 inches in length; a plank 20–28 inches long without splinters and with rounded corners; gym mats

Instructions: Putting a piece of wood on a tube and balancing on it is easier said than done! You will definitely need an assistant when the children are practicing this game. The assistant stretches out her arms to guide the person onto the plank, which at first will have one end on the floor and the other pointing in the air. The participant first needs to get his balance on the plank. Practice first with the tube on a gym mat so that it won't roll too fast or too wildly. Make sure no one is standing next to the plank as it can shoot out of control if the person is not standing on it firmly.

Variation: Once the children have mastered the art of standing on the plank, they can add something more—juggling with balls for instance, or balancing something on their heads.

Note: Safety is of the utmost importance, and you should be careful when gauging if this game is suitable for your particular situation.

The Ladder

Props: An aluminum ladder 6–8 feet high; gym mats

Instructions: Walking a tightrope 3 feet from the ground is not very exciting for 10-year-olds. Climbing a ladder by yourself without anyone holding the ladder is an art and worth a round of applause. Make sure that extra assistants are on hand to catch or help people if they get in a difficult spot. The participants should climb one rung at a time, placing their feet at the center of each rung. Participants should try it first while people are holding the ladder on each side. (The people holding the ladder should support it with their legs bent.) Then each child can try climbing the ladder by himself.

Moving around on the ladder is another trick that is possible after lots of practice.

Note: Safety is of the utmost importance, and you should be careful when gauging if this game is suitable for your particular situation.

Three Ladders

Props: Three aluminum ladders 8 feet high; gym mats; a paper parasol

Instructions: Two vertical ladders serve as a stand for the third ladder, which is secured horizontally between them at a certain height. The ladder structure needs to be steady and secure, preferably attached by ropes to other stationary structures if not also held in place by assistants.

One participant steps along the horizontal ladder, at a height of 7 feet or less. Once the children master this, they can try walking with the help of a paper parasol in one hand.

Variation: If the stunt works well, you could let other participants climb on the assistants and do a trick while the first participant works on the ladder itself.

Tip: Make sure that the assistants stand with legs bent. Standing with knees locked, a person can lose her balance more easily when reacting to an unexpected fast movement.

Note: Safety is of the utmost importance, and you should be careful when gauging if this game is suitable for your particular situation.

Scooter or Tricycle?

Props: A scooter or tricycle; costumes

Instructions: Children ages 10 and over love to do stunts on their bikes. At this age, they also want their bikes to look sporty with special tires and other eye-catching accessories. But the most eye-catching thing is when someone does a "wheelie."

This first exercise is done on the scooter or tricycle because it is less dangerous than on a bicycle and because it is a great way to do some spectacular tricks. Even entering the ring to music, dressed in special costumes, in a column or other formation, can be an act in itself.

Here, too, you don't need to add a lot of extras to make the act interesting: clothing, the scooter nicely decorated, and an extra flourish that no one expects. For example, some scooters have a brake system that makes it possible to stop the scooter almost vertically. And a tricycle show can look good, especially if the participants are too big for them but use their size to perform some special stunts on the tricycle.

Note: Safety is of the utmost importance, and you should be careful when gauging if this game is suitable for your particular situation.

10+

DANGER

Bike Act

Props: Sporty bikes; costumes

Music: Music appropriate to the routine, not longer than 2–3 minutes

Tip: This act should be performed in a gym or outside, if possible.

Instructions: For a bike act, participants can do stunts similar to those they would do on a scooter. Bicycles are a bit less maneuverable than scooters; have riders work out the choreography first and then practice it on the performance site.

Some ideas:

- Depending on the size of the performance space, work out how many bikes can come on and off at the same time.

- Make patterns that begin simply and can get more complicated as the music plays.

- Pay attention to the costumes and how easy/difficult they will be while riding a bicycle.

- Think of using the bike act as a finale with a special balancing act standing on the bikes at the end.

Note: Safety is of the utmost importance, and you should be careful when gauging if this game is suitable for your particular situation.

Roller Skates

Props: Roller skates, inline skates; a special surface

Music (optional): Music appropriate to the routine

Instructions: Much has changed about roller skates in recent years. As everyone knows from seeing roller skaters either on television or at a live performance, just as with ice skating, a revolution has occurred: People are much more inventive with their routines, there are many more separate tricks, and they have much more effect on the public.

The old-fashioned skates do not exist anymore and modern designs allow skaters to do far more than before. Skating in formation or one behind the other, skating in pairs—anything is possible. To incorporate a roller skate act into the circus, focus on good choreography and well-chosen music. This will help create a real spectacle.

Ask the participants to consider the following:

1. *How many people will be needed for the act?*

2. *What kind of skates are best for the surface available?*

3. *What would be suitable music and how long should it be?*

4. *What should the choreography consist of?*

5. *What type of finale would be good? Perhaps something special can be added or two acts can be combined? For example, consider combining this act/choreography with balls or rings.*

Pyramid for Six

Props: A soft floor covering such as mats

Music (optional): Music appropriate to the routine

Instructions: Build a human pyramid! First, have three children kneel down in a row close to each other. Two children then kneel on the shoulders of those on the bottom row, and one more climbs up to kneel on the shoulders of those two.

The children at the edges can hold one hand out sideways and link the other arm with the child beside them. The child at the top of the pyramid can hold both arms out when everyone else is steady. At this age, the children can add these touches on a signal or in rhythm with the music. Then everyone stays frozen still for several counts to give the audience time to applaud.

Notes:

- Make sure the children practice how to dismount from the pyramid.
- Safety is of the utmost importance, and you should be careful when gauging if this game is suitable for your particular situation.

Clowns and Music

Props: Two clown noses; wigs; various instruments such as a large drum, trumpet, or gong

Instructions: Some instruments immediately conjure up pictures of a clown act. Consider the tuba, the big drum, the trumpet, and the gong.

This book includes plenty of clowning games and acts, and with this age group you can take these one step farther and accompany an act with live music. Bang on the drum when a clown gets hit in the backside, for instance; strike a gong when he walks into the wall and sees stars...maybe adding a little twiddle on the flute.

Divide the class into groups of four with two clowns and two musicians per group. Each group thinks up an act lasting about one minute and figures out what sounds can add an important element to the act.

Think of short story lines with which to introduce the clowns. As we get to know them, we can quickly see their shortcomings which are sure to lead to some disaster! But all's well that ends well, and that, too, can be emphasized with the instruments.

After 25 minutes, the groups can present their acts to the class. The groups can advise each other how to make each act better and what sounds still need working on.

The **Limbo**

Props: A bamboo pole 7 feet in length

Music: South American or Caribbean music to stir up the excitement

Tip: This act should be performed outside, if possible.

Instructions: Everyone knows this act: Two people hold a bamboo pole at chest height so that someone can dance under, bowing backward just a little. Each time a participant goes through, the pole is lowered a bit. A dancer is not allowed to stop once she has started moving; the dance has to be done in one smooth movement, even when the person reaches the pole. Who can dance under the pole when it is held at 20 inches from the ground...or lower?

This act works best outdoors in the sunshine when the sand is dry, warm, and loose. The music sweeps the dancer along as the audience cheers her on.

Trampoline

Props: A trampoline; mats; instruments

Instructions: Many schools have a trampoline. It can be used to jump onto or over the horse. Of course, on a trampoline you can also jump over other people; perhaps one person jumps and the others dive out of the way. The children will imagine all kinds of possibilities. The trampoline can also be used to catapult people over or behind a curtain where we just caught a glimpse of someone.

You need very little more to make this a very amusing act, including screaming and the crash of pots and pans to make the disaster appear still worse.

Divide the class into groups of five people. The groups will work together for 25 minutes to create and rehearse their ideas. Each act should last a minute or two and have a climax. Which group can think up the best act, with the widest variety of yells and sounds?

This is also a great game to use as a clown act. Who can come out 30 seconds after the jump all wrinkled and crinkled? Or maybe they get carried in sitting in a pie?

Note: For jumps that go offstage, assistants need to be ready to catch the jumper.

Handstand Chain

Lots of children can do handstands at this age. They may not be able to hold the pose for very long, but many can manage some attempt.

Instructions: Have a group of children stand together in a line. At your signal, alternate children go into handstands, quickly switching from feet to hands. The child next to each performer supports him or her. At another signal, the children reverse roles, so that the entire line of children alternates between standing on their feet and standing on their hands. The chain of standing and hand standing keeps changing and could follow the beat of the music as well as signals from you.

Variation: After several switches from feet to hands, the people doing handstands walk away from the chain on their hands.

On the Rings

Props: Rings; mats; music

Instructions: A set of rings is a standard piece of equipment in the gym. If your setup has them, devote one or more classes to teaching the kids to hang and swing on the rings, with help if necessary.

Notes:

1. Always have the class warm up before attempting any exercises on the rings; arm and leg exercises are particularly important here.
2. Hang the rings no higher than the children can reach easily.
3. Always check the rings and ropes before you start.
4. Make sure to lay plenty of mats under the rings where the children will land (or could fall).
5. Make sure the children agree not to jump across each other.
6. The leader and any assistants should stay by the rings at all times.

Using the rings to swing and jump can be practiced easily, but jumping over an obstacle such as a gym horse or with something on your head requires a little more work.

Safety is of the utmost importance, and you should be careful when gauging if this game is suitable for your particular situation. Watch out for children being overconfident about what they say they can do. And remember that even stunts they say they know might be dangerous. Children who do acrobatics may be especially overconfident and do a somersault or something similar on the rings. Put that action into the program only if that participant can do it well.

Tip: A gym teacher makes a good assistant in this game as he will be familiar with the apparatus.

Walking Money

Prop: A coin

Instructions: Explain this trick to the children and let them practice it for themselves. Children at this age love practicing a trick like this until they can do it well. If some of the children seem especially taken with this, you can find many other conjuring tricks, such as cards, at party or joke shops.

Lead the children by saying the following:

- *For this trick, choose a coin that's not too heavy.*
- *Make a fist with your right hand.*
- *Hold the thumb next to your index finger.*
- *Place a coin over the thumb and index finger.*
- *By making up and down movements with your fingers, you can make the coin "walk" across your fist.*
- *When the coin gets to the end of your hand, let it slip between your fingers and catch it with your thumb and begin again.*

Variation: Let the coin roll back across your fist the other way.

Thimble

Props: A thimble; a suit jacket

Instructions: Teach the children this tricky movement:

Put a thimble on your index finger. Pretend that you are taking off the thimble under your coat and putting it under your left arm. Show everyone that the thimble is off your finger. They will think it is under your arm.

Hold your hand behind your head and then show it again. The thimble is back on your finger!

   Solution: *Put another thimble in your collar and practice putting it on quickly.*

Another solution is that you actually move the thimble into your fist. Then, when you put your hand behind your head, it magically appears on your finger again.

Ball and Cloth

Props: Pieces of silk 16 × 16 inches; small balls, around 1 inch in diameter

Instructions: Tell the children that the ball and cloth is another well-known trick. Lead them through the following steps:

- *Let the audience see and feel the ball and cloth, so they know that both are real.*
- *Lay the cloth so that it covers your right fist.*
- *Make a little hollow, pushing the cloth into your fist, where you can hide the ball. Drop the ball into the cloth. At the same time as you catch it in the cloth and tuck it away, the ball you already had in your fist drops out. The audience will want to know how that ball got out!*

The art of conjuring lies in distracting the viewer's attention. You draw the audience to look at one thing while you do something else. In this case, flourishing waves with the silk cloth kept their attention on you and the first ball. They never saw the second ball until it dropped from your hand.

Three Cigar Boxes

Props: Three cigar boxes

Instructions: First, of course, you need to find the boxes. That's no longer as easy as it used to be. Who still smokes? Especially, who smokes those great fat cigars that come in the sturdy kind of cigar box.

Tape each box firmly closed. If you want to, you could fill them with bubble wrap or polystyrene. Make sure that each box weighs the same. Now walk the participants through these steps:

- *Hold the three boxes together at waist level; draw your hands slightly apart and let the middle box fall.*

- *Catch it again quickly between the other two boxes.*

It won't always work. It is like the shell game; participants have to be really fast.

Tommy Cooper (see page 67) would probably have managed to glue all three boxes together, or put a magnet inside them!

On Your Hands (Wheelbarrow)

Props (optional): Wheels with handles of some kind

Instructions: Divide the group into pairs of children. Have each pair practice together. The idea is simple: one of the children walks on her hands while her partner holds her legs in the air.

Tip: The participant holding the other's legs should start by taking one ankle and then the other. When the pair comes to a stop, they should follow the same procedure, putting down first one foot and then the other.

Variations:

- A variation on this theme is to place some object on the back of the one walking on his hands—the wheelbarrow—a bowl of water, for instance.

- Putting an obstacle in the pair's path can also be fun, particularly if this involves changing levels.

- An even more interesting variation is when the person on his hands holds a wheel between his hands so he can be steered along. This is quite tricky, so start slowly. Remember that people could fall hard on their faces.

92

Frisbee Throwers

Props: Frisbees (most families have a Frisbee at home somewhere—usually in some bright color)

Tip: This act should be performed outside, if possible.

Instructions: The Frisbee throwers are four circus performers who can throw several Frisbees at the same time, spinning around with each throw. That's the final aim, anyway!

Begin simply, having two people throwing and catching one Frisbee. Help the children figure out the best distance to be able to do a good throw. These performers can also perform for the public outside and do their tricks. Once everyone has the knack of throwing one Frisbee, participants can work with more than one at the same time and use different body movements.

Let the group who is going to perform make a sketch of what they plan to do. Dress everyone in yellow—the same color as the Frisbee—or in a contrasting color.

The Beach-Ball Slammers

Props: Tennis rackets; tennis balls

Instructions: The Beach-Ball Slammers are holding auditions for children wanting to join their act. Split the group into pairs of children. Each pair then practices together, batting the ball back and forth to each other. The pair with the most hits back and forth in the time allotted goes on to the next round.

Keeping the ball aloft becomes the next challenge. Which pair can hit the ball back and forth, without letting it hit the ground, for the longest? Along with the class, come up with different challenges for the players who are auditioning to be a part of this act.

Caterpillar

Props: Gym mats

Instructions: Every child can roll. As noted earlier, it is best to roll over the shoulder rather than head and neck. However, for this roll—called the caterpillar—participants need to roll over the head. Divide the class into pairs and work through the following steps:

- *Number 1 lies on his back on the ground.*
- *Number 2 stands with his legs next to Number 1's ears.*
- *Number 1 raises his legs.*
- *Number 2 grabs Number 1's ankles and Number 1 grabs Number 2's ankles.*
- *Number 2 does a somersault between Number 1's legs, placing his hands and Number 1's feet as close to Number 1's bottom as possible and supporting his own arms on the floor.*
- *As Number 2 goes down in his roll, Number 1 comes up, because he is holding Number 2's feet. He then goes into his own roll, remembering to place his hands and Number 2's feet close to Number 2's bottom, and the partners continue in this way.*

Shadowy Dreams

Props: A large sheet or piece of cheesecloth, at least as big as a double bed sheet; lamp

Music: Music appropriate to the routine

Instructions: With sheet and lamp, participants can create an interesting shadow act. Start by hanging the sheet so it is taut or have two people hold it. Place the lamp at some distance from the sheet so the participants have enough room to move toward the sheet to do their shadow-play. Most any lamp will work, but a lamp with a focused beam—like a spotlight—works best.

Tell the children to stand sideways to the sheet when possible. If they directly face the sheet, the audience cannot see the facial features. Also, demonstrate for them that the closer you come to the sheet, the smaller and sharper your shape becomes. The farther away you are, the larger and vaguer you become.

In a circus act, use this game to show things that are not possible to show in any other way—a many-headed monster, a many-armed monster, or even a dream sequence.

Smoke can also add to the atmosphere if you can lay hands on a smoke machine.

Cossack Dance

Props: Clothing (see description below)

Music: Cossack music, or Russian or Eastern European folk music

Instructions: At this age, children will be able to learn and perform the Cossack dance. The International Dance Theater has a Cossack dance in many of their programs. Everyone recognizes it at once, though few of the class will have seen it live.

In this dance, a dancer crosses his arms in front of his chests and then kicks his feet out in front of himself one at a time, from a crouching position. For the performance it is advisable to dress the children as Cossacks, with half-length pants, jacket, cap, ballet shoes or boots.

A group of dancers can dance solo, or, still in a crouching position, they can take each other by the shoulders and dance together in a row. Choreograph the dance: how will dancers come on, how will they perform the dance, and finally how will they exit?

Fantastic Announcements

Props: Paper; pens; a copy machine; a microphone; a speaker installation

Music: Circus or marching band music

Instructions: A good program leaflet has lots of text and some good photos. Enhance what the audience has in their hands, however, by making announcements about the acts they will see even as they take their seats. This is a great way to warm up the audience while they wait for the first act. And between acts, it entices people to stay.

With the children, write about the animals and performers who are not appearing today, as well as those who will definitely be performing. Read the announcements over a microphone with circus music playing in the background. The texts should start with the simple announcement of what is happening today and lead to a climax.

Examples:

- "Today, it is not the one-legged pig on the trapeze that will amaze you, but the miniature giraffe on the perilous scooter."

- "A troupe of acrobats traveled here all the way from Thailand to perform their fantastic act—the multiperson pyramid, complete with thirty-six acrobats. Unfortunately some of the acrobats appear to have gotten lost in the city, so instead we are bringing you something completely different...."

Playback Show

Props: Music installation; a make-believe microphone; costumes

Music: Songs great for lip-syncing performances

Instructions: Lip-syncing to a singer or a band has been a favorite act for many years, particularly for younger children. This form of entertainment is not highly regarded, but it is great fun. The act could consist of a single performer lip-synching a favorite singer. But you could also have a whole team of people "singing" a medley like this—each performing one song. The important thing is to choose participants who really enjoy doing this and who can truly get into the part and become complete doubles of the musicians they choose to imitate. The more "over the top" the performance is, the more fun it will be to watch.

Ribbon Dancers

Props: A wooden stick with 7 feet of wide satin ribbon (about 1 inch wide) attached for each participant

Music: Music appropriate to the routine

A performance by ribbon dancers can be a good way to get the audience in the mood.

Instructions: Many people have seen ribbon dancers at the Olympic Games. Younger children—girls in particular—enjoy this activity. For the circus, each participant has a stick with a ribbon on it. Dancers move together, keeping the ribbons moving as they do.

Introduce and practice the basics first; then try out patterns and add a dance. Walk the children through the following:

1. *Make a waving movement with the stick.*

2. *Make up-and-down movements.*

3. Feel the difference between large and small movements.

4. Try to make the ribbons dance across you.

5. Try to dance as well, while still keeping the ribbon moving.

6. Try to pick up the stick and ribbon from the floor in a dance movement.

7. With all dancers together, dance to a short piece of music. Try to create a dance that focuses on the ribbon. Decide first how to do it so you don't get tangled in someone else's ribbon.

Chinese Plates

Props: Plastic plates with an edge and indentation on the underside; sticks about 3 feet in length, with a sharpened point at one end

This act comes from China. If you see it at the circus, the artiste starts by spinning a plate on the end of a stick and before you know it there are twenty plates spinning. Participants of this age enjoy learning this trick; it takes a lot of practice but is not really difficult.

Instructions: Hang the plate on the stick. Hold the stick firmly, placing your forefinger against the stick. Hold the stick straight and make circles in the air with the point. (You can also try to spin the plate in the other direction with thumb and index finger.)

Try to make the movement from the wrist.

Try to go faster. The faster you go, the straighter the plate will spin.

Variations:

- Begin by demonstrating how to get the plate spinning and pass it around the circle.

- Participants can take the plate over onto their own sticks and continue passing the plate this way.

Barrel Roll

Props: A small heavy wooden spool, as from electrical wire; gym mats

Tip: This act should be performed outside, if possible.

Many people have seen clowns or lions or other animals rolling atop a ball at the circus. With a little practice, the children will enjoy a similar act that showcases balance work or serves as a good base for a clown act.

Instructions: Locate a sturdy wooden spool of the kind used for electrical wire. Once emptied of wire, these spools are excellent for balance walking. Demonstrate for the children how, with the help of an assistant, you can mount the spool. Show them first the idea of just getting your balance while standing on top. Next begin walking slowly, moving the spool beneath your feet. Dismount in the same way as you got on.

Have the children take turns trying their balance on the spool. Remind them to work on balance even as they begin rolling the spool.

Note: Safety is of the utmost importance, and you should be careful when gauging if this game is suitable for your particular situation.

Recommended Books, Sources for Materials, and Music

Books

Rooyackers, Paul. *101 Drama Games for Children.* Alameda, CA: Hunter House Publishers, 1998.

Rooyackers, Paul. *101 More Drama Games for Children.* Alameda, CA: Hunter House Publishers, 2002.

Bedore, Bob. *101 Improv Games for Children and Adults.* Alameda, CA: Hunter House Publishers, 2004.

Sources for Materials

Karaoke Music

www.pocketsongs.com

www.world-of-karaoke.com

Props

www.jugglingstore.com

www.in-tent.com

Music

Benoit Jutras—*Cirque du Soleil: Mystère*

René DuPéré—*Cirque du Soleil: Alegría*

Bernard Noly—*Sur la Piste du Cirque*

Eastman Wind Ensemble—*Screamers (Circus Marches)*

Saint-Saëns—*Le Carnival des Animaux*

Music from the films of Charlie Chaplin

Music from the films of Laurel and Hardy

Music by Nino Rota

Alphabetical List of Games

The Games Arranged by Specific Categories

Games Requiring an Assistant

6. Balance
7. I Can Fly
9. Conveyor Belt
10. The Worm
11. What Animal Is This?
12. Elastic Jersey Dancers
13. Rolling
14. Tricks with the Balance Beam
15. Out of Balance
16. Two Clowns
17. The Big Bench
18. On Top of Each Other
19. Boxes
20. The Best Box-Stacking Clown
21. A Course in Falling
22. Falling with Boxes
23. Falling into the Box
24. The Oversized Coat or Sweater
25. A Bucket of Water
26. Rope
28. Circus School Obstacle Course
29. Two Ladders and a Bench
37. Elastic
63. Stilt Walkers
75. Rolling Plank
76. The Ladder
77. Three Ladders
81. Pyramid for Six
84. Trampoline
86. On the Rings
94. Caterpillar
101. Barrel Roll

Game Requiring a Large Space

1. Warming Up
2. What's the Idea?
3. Antonio Macaroni's Circus Family
4. The Chair Act from Napoli
5. Look! No Hands!
6. Balance
7. I Can Fly
8. I Know a Trick
9. Conveyor Belt
10. The Worm
11. What Animal Is This?
12. Elastic Jersey Dancers
13. Rolling
14. Tricks with the Balance Beam
15. Out of Balance
16. Two Clowns
17. The Big Bench
18. On Top of Each Other
19. Boxes
20. The Best Box-Stacking Clown
21. A Course in Falling
22. Falling with Boxes
23. Falling into the Box
24. The Oversized Coat or Sweater
25. A Bucket of Water

Games in Which Physical Contact Might Be Involved

Games Requiring Props

Games Requiring Musical Accompaniment

101 MUSIC GAMES FOR CHILDREN: Fun and Learning with Rhythm and Song by Jerry Storms

All you need to play these games are music CDs and simple instruments, many of which kids can make from common household items. Many games are good for large group settings, such as birthday parties, others are easily adapted to classroom needs. No musical knowledge is required. **Ages 4 and up.**

>> 160 pages ... 30 illus. ... Paperback $14.95 ... Spiral bound $19.95

101 DANCE GAMES FOR CHILDREN: Fun and Creativity with Movement by Paul Rooyackers

These games encourage children to interact and express how they feel in creative ways, without words. They include meeting and greeting games, cooperation games, story dances, party dances, "musical puzzles," dances with props, and more. No dance training or athletic skills are required. **Ages 4 and up.**

>> 160 pages ... 36 illus. ... Paperback $14.95 ... Spiral bound $19.95

101 DRAMA GAMES FOR CHILDREN: Fun and Learning with Acting and Make-Believe by Paul Rooyackers

Drama games are a fun, dynamic form of play that help children explore their imagination and creativity. These noncompetitive games include introduction games, sensory games, pantomime games, story games, sound games, games with masks, games with costumes, and more. The "play-ful" ideas help to develop self-esteem, improvisation, communication, and trust. **Ages 4 and up.**

>> 160 pages ... 30 illus. ... Paperback $14.95 ... Spiral bound $19.95

101 IMPROV GAMES FOR CHILDREN ... by Bob Bedore

Improv comedy has become very popular, and this book offers the next step in drama and play: a guide to creating something out of nothing, reaching people using talents you didn't know you possessed. Contains exercises for teaching improv to children, advanced improv techniques, and tips for thinking on your feet — all from an acknowledged master of improv. **Ages 5 and up.**

>> 192 pages ... 65 b/w photos ... Paperback $14.95 ... Spiral bound $19.95

THE YOGA ADVENTURE FOR CHILDREN: Playing, Dancing, Moving, Breathing, Relaxing by Helen Purperhart

Offers an opportunity for the whole family to laugh, play, and have fun together. This book for children 4–12 years old explains yoga stretches and postures as well as the philosophy behind yoga. The exercises are good for a child's mental and physical development, and also improve concentration and self-esteem. **Ages 4–12.**

>> 144 pages ... 75 illus. ... Paperback $14.95 ... Spiral bound $19.95